THE EMOTIONALLY DESTRUCTIVE RELATIONSHIP:

"Here is a book I deeply wish didn't need to be written, but also one I am so grateful Leslie Vernick has had the courage to write. You will be moved by her compassion, be appreciative of her candor, and be helped by her professional skills honed in the trenches of real life."

—**Gene Appel,** Lead Pastor, Willow Creek Community Church,
South Barrington, Illinois

✳

"If you have been wounded or trapped in a destructive relationship, you are not alone. Your life story isn't over. These are the life-transforming themes of hope that Leslie affirms as she shares her healing journey."

—**Dr. Catherine Hart Weber,**
coauthor of *Secrets of Eve* and *Unveiling Depression in Women;*
Fuller Theological Seminary adjunct professor

✳

"I could relate to so many of the people mentioned in this book, and it really scared me...I knew I had to make changes in my life and marriage...

"Leslie uses Scripture to validate the points she makes, which is different than any of the other books I have read...I would highly recommend this book to anyone who is in or has been in an emotionally destructive relationship. It has changed my outlook on myself and my marriage."

—**Jess,** a reader

✳

"This book is a must-read—not only will it educate the reader to take the necessary steps to freedom, but it will also prevent future destructive relationships."

—**Michelle Borquez**
author of *God Crazy: An Adventurous Road Trip to Joyful Surrender*
Host of I-Life TV's *Shine*

Lord, I Just Want to Be Happy

Leslie Vernick

HARVEST HOUSE PUBLISHERS
EUGENE, OREGON

Cover by Dugan Design Group, Bloomington, Minnesota

Cover photo © Blend Images Photography / Veer

Back cover photo of author © Sally Ullman Photography

LORD, I JUST WANT TO BE HAPPY
Copyright © 2009 by Leslie Vernick
Published by Harvest House Publishers
Eugene, Oregon 97402
www.harvesthousepublishers.com

Library of Congress Cataloging-in-Publication Data

Vernick, Leslie.
Lord, I just want to be happy / Leslie Vernick.
   p. cm.
Includes bibliographical references.
ISBN 978-0-7369-1923-4 (pbk.)
ISBN 978-0-7369-3612-5 (eBook)
1. Happiness—Religious aspects—Christianity. I. Title.
BV4647.J68V475 2009
248.4—dc22
                                                                2009024274

Printed in the United States of America

14 15 16 17 18 19 20 / BP-NI / 13 12 11 10 9 8 7 6 5 4

· · · · · · · · · · · · · · · · · · ·

*I pray...that you may be filled to the
measure of all the fullness of God.*

PAUL, IN EPHESIANS 3:17,19

· · · · · · · · · · · · · · · · · · ·

Acknowledgments

Each book I have written is like a pregnancy. It starts as a small seed and miraculously grows larger and larger over months of reflection, thinking, reading, and prayer. For me, the birthing process of writing out my thoughts is a long, hard, and excruciatingly painful labor. There were moments when I was tempted to give up, call it quits, and allow my precious baby to die in the womb. I am especially grateful for my prayer team, AWSA sisters, and special friends who did not let that happen. Although my name is on the cover, please know that without your prayers and your encouragement, I would not have had the strength to push out this book.

I am also thankful for my editor, Paul Gossard at Harvest House Publishers, who not only has worked hard to clean up my baby and make it more beautiful, but went to bat for me when it looked like the birthing process would take a little more time than we thought. Your kindness and understanding comforted and strengthened me and gave me that little extra I needed to persevere.

To my friends and colleagues Georgia Shaffer, Erin Stephens, Glenna Dameron, and Howard Lawler, I deeply appreciate that you have taken your valuable time to read through my early chapters and give me your helpful comments. As a benefit, I hope you have gained some insights and new skills in enhancing your own happiness levels.

Thank you, Donna Barats—my office manager—who went to the library, searched the Internet, kept all my books and notes straightened out, and took care of everything else while I was preoccupied and unavailable. Michele Boynton, you go over and above the call of duty, and I could not do my work if you did not help me as you do.

Howard, Ryan, and Amanda, you bless me and keep me honest and real.

Last, but never least, thank you, Lord, for the strength you gave me. Without your sustaining grace, immeasurable wisdom, and profound love, I would be lost and most miserable.

Contents

God Has Designed
You for Happiness

I WANT YOU TO KNOW that you were made to be happy.

It's true. God wants us to feel hope, joy, love, and peace. These are wonderful feelings, not theological concepts. We were created to live in faith and love, not in fear and bondage. God designed our body, our brain, our emotions, and our spirit to thrive when we live in sync with him and our created purpose.

However, instead of living as God ordained, seeing him as our center and source for life, we have sought our happiness in god-substitutes. The problem is not with our longing. That is built right into our natures. Our problem is with what we think will satisfy that longing. John Piper, pastor and author of *Desiring God,* says, "We all make a god out of what we take the most pleasure in."[1] We can all relate. We've been deceived by lesser pleasures. Instead of hungering after God, we've feasted at the table of cheap substitutes. No wonder we are left still hungry and longing for more.

❦

In conversations and in reading about the essence of a happy heart, I have found it is not easily defined. When someone feels deep-down happy, I believe she feels fully alive—aware of herself, others, and life. She has a zest for living. Truly happy people are attuned to God, in tune with themselves, and grateful for life. It doesn't mean they don't feel pain, hurt, or sorrow, but they don't hang on to those feelings longer than necessary. The more fully alive you are, the more you will feel and experience life in both its positive and negative apsects. Jesus felt joy and happiness, yet he is described as a man of sorrows, acquainted with grief.

Recently my dear friend Theresa lost her brother to breast cancer. At his funeral she opened his eulogy with the statement, "I have learned that life isn't about either/or, it's about both/and." She continued to describe both the tremendous beauty and heart-wrenching pain she experienced throughout her brother's illness. She spoke about the hard aspects and the good ones, the horrible as well as the lovely. Life and death. Good and bad. Strong and weak. Joy and sorrow. She felt happy *and* sad all at the same time.

True inner happiness doesn't involve the absence of pain. The happy person doesn't deny her inner ache, but is able to embrace suffering *and* transform it so it doesn't become crippling or deadening. Life often contains a *yea* and an *ugh*...all at the same time. One of my clients who has felt depressed much of his life told me, "I was desperately unhappy when I felt nothing. Pain at least let me know I was alive. My pain was good because it brought me to God."*

---

* Client stories have been disguised and details altered to protect the identity of individuals.

Aiming Toward Happiness

Longing for happiness has gotten a bad rap in some Christian circles. We've seen it as shallow, temporal, and self-centered, not characteristic of a mature believer's desires. Yet Blaise Pascal, the Christian philosopher and mathematician wrote,

> All look for happiness without exception. Although they use different means, they all strive toward this objective. That is why some go to war and some do other things. So this is the motive for every deed of man, including those who hang themselves.[2]

C.S. Lewis, writing to a friend said, "It is a Christian duty, as you know, for everyone to be as happy as he can."[3] We have not only minimized the importance of happiness to our overall well-being, we've secularized it. Recently I spoke with Jennifer, a young woman who told me she just couldn't be happy unless she was at a certain weight and had lots of money to spend.

We've allowed our well-being and happiness to be contingent upon getting something from this world. We've not grasped that lasting happiness has more to do with the way our internal world is oriented than what we get from temporal pleasures. Heartfelt happiness isn't found in fun places, sinful pleasure, popularity, productivity, power, or prestige. Rather it is the result of right (truthful) thinking, right relationships, right choices, and right living. Happiness is not something we receive; it is something we *become* as we love God and live our lives enjoying him and his creation and growing in his wisdom.

For some of you, these ideas may sound new and are hard to grasp. Francine came to see me for counseling because she felt unhappy with her life. She had been married for close to 35 years. Most of them had been difficult. In a light moment, she remarked, "I've always had a C-minus marriage, some years I'd even give it a D-minus. How can

I be happy? I'll never have the kind of relationship with my husband I've always longed for."

People like Francine and Jennifer are not alone. We all get disappointed when we don't get what we want, especially when we believe that what we want is essential to our well-being. Everyone has desires, longings, and wants. They're not all the same, but they're all important to us. Perhaps your desire is to look a certain way or to have a good marriage. Others long for more money so they can pay their bills on time and maybe have a little left over once in a while for some recreation. Or you may already have a good job, but crave greater success, more affirmation, or more appreciation from people. Maybe you only want a clean house and obedient kids for a change. You're not asking for the moon—you'd be happy with a few ordinary pleasures.

Don't get me wrong. A good marriage, adequate financial resources, even a clean home and well-behaved children do bring some measure of happiness. However, temporal blessings, as wonderful as they may be, are only a taste of the real thing. They cannot sustain inner happiness any more than eating a scrumptious meal keeps tomorrow's hunger at bay. They don't satisfy us completely because they were never meant to. David declared that God himself was the source of his happiness. He said,

> My choice is you, God, first and only. And now I find I'm *your* choice! You set me up with a house and yard. And then you made me your heir! The wise counsel God gives when I'm awake is confirmed by my sleeping heart. Day and night I'll stick with God; I've got a good thing going and I'm not letting go. I'm happy from the inside out, and from the outside in. I'm firmly formed. You canceled my ticket to hell—that's not my destination! Now you've got my feet on the life path, all radiant from the shining of your face. Ever since you took my hand, I'm on the right way (Psalm 16:5-9 MSG).

Francine may never have a happy marriage, and you probably won't have everything your heart longs for either, but you *can* be a happier person. I want to show you how. Jesus reminded his disciples again and again that they were to abide in his love. That is the only thing that will never disappoint us. Jesus said, "I have told you these things so that you will be filled with my joy. Yes, your joy will overflow!" (John 15:11 NLT).

God wants us to rest in his love and to know *how* to handle difficult relationships and life circumstances in a productive, constructive, and hopeful way. His Word teaches us how to release our toxic emotions and shows us ways to overcome evil with good. Imagine how your life would be if you were no longer controlled by your negative emotions or bad moods. What would be different if your heart was filled with hope, joy, love, and peace instead of anxiety, despair, frustration, and hurt? Envision a life of meaning and purpose. That's what God wants for you.

• • • • • • • Do We Need Some Training? • • • • • • •

Recently I purchased a brand-new computer with all the bells and whistles that make it capable of some amazing work like complicated databases and top-notch brochures. I haven't produced anything too amazing yet. The problem isn't the computer—it's me. I don't know how to use what's available. I know only the basics, and without some training, I will never be able to access my computer's fullest capabilities.

The same thing is often true of our spiritual life. The apostle Peter writes that God has given us everything we need for life and godliness (2 Peter 1:3), but we don't know how to tap into the tremendous resources God has given us for living an abundant life. How do we abide in his love? How do we let go of our negative feelings and bad moods? How do we feel peace and experience joy even in the midst of difficult circumstances?

• •

Steps Toward Lasting Change

Over my years as a Christian counselor, I've repeatedly asked myself two questions. What makes people happy? And why, even as believers living with many privileges and blessings, do we feel grumpy, stressed, guilty, depressed, and disappointed so much of the time? *Lord, I just want to be happy* is a prayer whispered not only by depressed and desperate people, but by all of us who want to learn to be happier than we presently are.

There are many good books on suffering and how to go through it in a godly way. There aren't many books written from a Christian perspective that teach us how to be happy. Let me start by saying that there is nothing that you can ever buy, earn, achieve, or receive, including finding a great spouse or winning the lottery, that will give you a happily-ever-after life. That is only in the fairy tales.

I also want to make a distinction between feeling good and feeling happy. They can go together. But we can also feel good using cocaine or indulging in some other sinful pleasure, but not necessarily feel happy. Optimists naturally feel happier than pessimists do, but their positive feelings may actually blind them to their inner emptiness and keep them content enough so they never seek the source of pure pleasure, lasting love, and true hope, which is in God alone.

Lord, I Just Want to Be Happy is divided into three parts. Part 1 is "Understanding Our Unhappiness." These chapters will help you identify the obstacles that keep you stuck in your own misery. I will explore our unrealistic expectations, bad habits, and the way we get caught in our negative thoughts and emotions, all leading us to make poor choices that hinder us from the wholeness and holiness Jesus calls us to. Throughout this part I will help you start to make small changes in order to acquire more positive emotions and inner well-being.

In part 2, "Moving Beyond Unhappiness," I want to help you learn God's road map for having a life well-lived and finding what he tells us brings joy, peace, hope, and contentment to our lives. I want you to fall in love, become more beautiful, and get into a training routine that will help you be holy and happy.

Lastly, in part 3, "Practicing Happiness," I will show you practical ways to build healthy habits into your daily life. Lasting change doesn't occur in leaps, but in tiny and faithful steps. Small changes can make a big difference. I'll show you the tools you'll need to find meaning in your life and how to transform a painful event, as well as how to build more positive emotions, such as gratitude, into your life.

A Vision for You

I used to think that it was God's will for us to be holy, not necessarily happy. But I don't believe that anymore. God surely calls us to be holy but he also made us to be happy. Holiness and happiness are not opposites but part of a whole. Holiness leads to wholeness and wholeness leads to happiness.

Holy people are happy people. They have found their source of joy, peace, love, and hope to be God and are living in sync with their created purpose. We will only experience what our soul craves when we pursue *God,* not happiness. Jesus tells us, "Blessed are those who hunger and thirst for righteousness, for they will be filled" (Matthew 5:6). When we are "in Christ" and Christ is "in us," we begin an incredible journey of healing and holiness (wholeness).

We now have the capacity to deeply love as we were designed to love. We are empowered to live in harmony with who we really are. Our thoughts and emotions become aligned and in tune instead of discordant and dissonant. We don't have to live at cross-purposes anymore with who we were made to be. We are free to become our true selves. Jesus intends this abundance for all believers everywhere, regardless of temperament, life circumstances, or family history.

Everybody I know wants to be happy or happier. But actually feeling happy for any sustained period of time is not as easy as we may think. For one thing, we battle with a real enemy who seeks to destroy us (John 10:10). If he can't stop our salvation, he will attempt to steal our joy and peace. He will try to confuse us as to what brings genuine happiness. In addition to Satan's schemes, living here on earth hurts. Things don't go our way. People let us down. Those we love don't love us back the way we want them to. Our financial future may be in peril and many Christians tell me they feel exhausted, overwhelmed, and too busy to enjoy their life. They don't experience the joy, love, peace, and inner well-being that God designed for us to have.

In my own quest for happiness, however, I have learned that the more I feel God's joy, peace, hope, and love the less I am looking for external life circumstances to make me happy. I have also observed in my own life as well as in the lives of many of my clients that, no matter how wonderful our external world may appear, if our internal world is a mess, we cannot feel happy.

As a counselor, I am well aware that many things are not as they should be. Sometimes living in this world is excruciatingly painful. It might be unrealistic to think we can be happy all of the time. But there are definitely some things we can learn so we can be happier people *more* of the time. Happiness is not simply a choice—it is also a skill we need to learn and practice regularly in order to maximize our ability to experience it. I am finally learning *how* to be a happier person, and you can too.

Questions for
• • • • •
Thought and Discussion

1. What kinds of things bring joy, hope, peace, and love to your daily life? Write them down. Do you tend to be intentional about cultivating these things, or do they "just happen" or not happen to you?

2. What do you think about the author's assertion that "happiness is first and foremost a mind-set...It is the result of right (truthful) thinking, right relationships, right choices, and right living" (page 13). Do you agree or disagree? Why or why not?

3. Read through Psalm 16 and Acts 2:26. What do you think David means when he says his heart is glad and his body will live in hope? Is that your normal experience, or do you often feel the more negative emotions in your body and heart?

4. Have you felt guilty or shallow for thinking or saying, "I just want to be happy"? How do you see holiness and happiness going together? How are they different?

5. Read John 10:10. The author states that "Jesus intends this abundance for all believers everywhere, regardless of your temperament, your life circumstances, or your family history." What are some specific examples from your own life or someone you know that indicate a person can be happy in spite of difficult life circumstances, a pessimistic temperament, or poor family history?

6. Do you look for the good things in the midst of negative circumstances, or do you get overwhelmed with the negative? Have
   you experienced both joy and heartache, a *yea* and an *ugh* at the
   same time?

7. What do you think of the idea that happiness is a skill we can
   learn?

PART ONE

• • • •

Understanding
Our Unhappiness

CHAPTER 1

Stories and Scripts

> *Do not seek to have events happen as you want*
> *them to, but instead want them to happen as*
> *they do happen, and your life will go well.*
>
> EPICTETUS 2

> *Expecting the world to treat you fairly because you*
> *are a good person is a little like expecting a bull not*
> *to attack you because you are a vegetarian.*
>
> DENNIS WHOLEY

JANET CAME INTO MY OFFICE UPSET, anxious to share her latest litany of what was wrong with her life. Her friend Dana hadn't invited her over last Sunday like Janet had hoped she would, and Janet felt hurt and rejected. Over the course of our counseling, I had learned that most of Janet's friends didn't support or love her as faithfully as she wished they would. She hated that she wasn't pretty enough, thin enough, or popular enough to gain the attention from others that she craved. Her job didn't satisfy her, nor did it pay enough, and the people there weren't very friendly either.

Janet's mother also irritated her. She described her mom as too busy living her own life to care that her daughter was a single mom and often needed help with her kids. That prompted me to ask Janet about her church family. She said she didn't get anything out of the sermons and no one from the Bible study ever invited her out to lunch—so why bother?

Janet wasn't clinically depressed, but she was miserable with herself, with others, and with life. If it wasn't one thing, it was another. Nothing was ever the way she wanted it to be, or the way it should be. "I just want to be happy," she moaned. "Why can't God make it easier for me? I hate that life is so hard, so unfair."

Perhaps your situation isn't as extreme as Janet's, but I think many of us can relate to her feelings. Life *does* disappoint us at times. Others don't give us the love or attention we want or expect, and as a result we feel angry, hurt, gypped, and sad. We hate that we're not perfect or popular or powerful or pretty enough to feel confident or attractive or worthy. Jesus' promise of an abundant life seems hollow. We get stuck living in a mind-set of, *If only I were more _____ or had more _____, then I'd be happy.* Or we tell ourselves, *If only _____ would change, then I could be happier.*

Take a minute and fill in the blanks for yourself. What might you put in? During one session, Janet said, "If only I were more popular and could lose ten pounds, then I'd be happy." At another session, she said something different: "If only my mother would change and help me out more with my kids, then I'd be happier."

What about you? Perhaps you tell yourself you'd be happy if only you were more beautiful, talented, or intelligent. Others say they'd be happy if only they had more money, more time, or more energy. You might believe you'd be happier if only you were married instead of single, or married to a different person instead of the one you're married to. Or maybe you'd rather not be married at all. Still others think that if only they had a baby, or better-behaved children, or a more attentive spouse, or a more prestigious or powerful job, or a bigger house, *then* they'd finally be happy.

Don't get me wrong. I'm all for making changes when possible and appropriate. But I've discovered in my own life, as well as in the lives of people I've worked with, that much of our misery is caused by the stories we tell ourselves about how things *should* be…rather than what actually is.

Unrealistic Expectations

Janet told herself that her unhappiness resulted from not being good enough, thin enough, or pretty enough. She was unhappy because she didn't make enough money, because people let her down, and because her life was unfair.

But those things weren't the true source of her suffering. Janet's misery was much more a result of her unrealistic expectations of herself, life, and others than of her actual life situations. Although she wasn't aware of it, Janet lived her life out of a mind-set, or way of thinking, that was largely false. She created an internal story line of how things *should* go—and when they didn't go the way she thought they should, she felt sorry for herself. For example, she believed life should be easy and fair. When life was hard, she found it impossible to handle her disappointment without falling into self-pity because, after all, life shouldn't be so hard.

Janet also told herself that people should be nicer to her and that they should be more willing to give of their time and efforts to help her out. She wasn't aware she did it, but she also scripted out what other people should say, how they should say it, and what they should do for her, especially if they claimed to be Christians. When they failed to follow her script, she felt hurt, disappointed, and angry with them. Not only that, but she also clung to those negative feelings for days, nursing more resentment and hurt.

But perhaps the biggest source of Janet's unhappiness was her own unrealistic view of herself. She regularly dwelled on her flaws and weaknesses and imagined that others did too. She fantasized she'd be more desirable, lovable, and popular if only she were thinner and more attractive.

In order for Janet to change and experience true happiness, she needs to become aware of the story line and scripts she has made up about herself, life, and others. Then she needs to reevaluate them according to what God says is true, good, and right. In addition, she must learn to handle the painful emotions that come with losses and disappointments in a different way, without falling into her habits of self-pity, resentment, or self-hatred.

You see, whether by nature we tend to look at the glass as half empty or half full, our perceptions determine our inner reality. By nature I am a pessimist, and because of that leaning, I often make up internal stories about the worst things that can happen. When my daughter started to drive, I made up all kinds of stories of dreadful accidents, carjackings, or mechanical failures. (None of which happened, I might add.) When my mammogram results came back suspicious, you can imagine where my mind went. As a result of my thinking habits, I often feel anxious, and my peace and inner sense of well-being vanish.

Optimists can make up some pretty unrealistic stories too. I once watched a man playing blackjack lose $20,000 thinking positively. He told himself (out loud) that this was his lucky day, he was *the* man, and tonight he'd strike it rich. He allowed his unrealistic story and script of how he wanted things to end to capture his heart, overrule his rational mind, and control his decision-making. (And in chapter 4, we'll see how a woman named Cheryl continued to believe her fantasy story line of a perfect fiancé—despite evidence to the contrary—only to wake up to an abusive husband.)

In order to learn how to be happier, we need to recognize 1) our internal stories and scripts and then 2) how they create expectations that, when unmet, often lead to foolish decisions as well as feeling anxious, miserable, sad, angry, discouraged, and even depressed.

Core Lies We Believe

There are many story lines and scripts that lead to misery and unhappiness, but the first clue in discovering your particular one is to look for the words *should, shouldn't, ought, supposed to,* and *deserve* and then listen to what comes next. Let's examine three of the most powerful ones.

"I should be better than I am"

Many people suffer because they fail to live up to their own expectations of themselves. Keith worked three part-time jobs just to put himself through college. He was proud of his accomplishments, but he started getting anxious and discouraged when some of his grades slipped from A's to B's and he fell behind in his rent payment. He studied long into the night, often forsaking sleep. He was cranky, exhausted, and definitely not happy.

But when I challenged his schedule, he insisted, "I should be able to handle this." He refused to accept reality. His self-concept was based on an idealized image of himself, not the truth. Keith is not a god—he is a mere mortal. He has limits. He can't function at his best with only four hours of sleep. He isn't able to work three jobs, study all night, sleep adequately, go to college full-time, and get straight A's in all of his subjects. Yet his expectations that he ought to be able to do it all, and his self-hatred for failing to live up to his idealized image of himself, was great.

People who are perfectionists may have a hard time admitting they actually expect they should be perfect all of the time, but deep down that's what they want to be. And they grieve deeply when they fail. They can never be happy, because although they might achieve a moment of perfection, it's unsustainable. Eventually they mess up, can't do something, aren't all-knowing, fail, or make a mistake. The internal shame, self-hatred, and self-reproach can be lethal.

Some individuals may not recognize they have unrealistic expectations of themselves, because they don't expect perfection in every area of their life. For example, Elle wasn't compulsive about her home, but she obsessed over her physical appearance. Every inch of her body and clothing had to look perfect, or she would beat herself up. "I shouldn't have eaten dinner last night" or, "I should exercise more, I'm so fat," she'd moan. She even slept with her makeup on so she would look good in the morning. No one was allowed to see her until she was ready, including her best friend.

• • • • • • • • • • • **Terminally Unique** • • • • • • • • • • • •

Cindy failed to live up to her idealized version of the perfect Christian wife and mother. In a moment of sin and passion, she committed adultery with a co-worker. Her sorrow was great, but her repentance shallow. Her grief was not because of her sin against her husband or against God, but because she became small in her own eyes for failing to live up to who she thought she was. "I can't believe I did that," Cindy lamented.

"Why is it so hard for you to accept you're a sinner, just like everyone else?" I asked.

"I don't want to be like everyone else," she replied.

"That's part of your problem," I gently told her. Much of Cindy's suffering was because she expected herself to be better than everyone else.

• •

People who believe they should be better than they are can't be happy, because they are morbidly preoccupied with themselves. They become prideful over their perfection or filled with self-hatred at their flaws.

As with Janet, one particular variation on the *I should be better than I am* story line is feeling disappointed with one's self over never being good enough, pretty enough, worthy enough, thin enough, spiritual enough, rich enough, or smart enough. You get the picture. The goal becomes *I want to be enough.* The question we must ask ourselves is, By whose yardstick will you measure yourself as "good enough"? Inevitably it is one's own standard, not God's. Even nonperfectionists like

Janet become self-conscious about their limitations, weaknesses, and flaws when they tell themselves that they shouldn't be that way, or if only they weren't that way, then they would be happy.

When we live by these scripts, we will never feel happy. We (or someone else) will always find some flaw. Let's be honest here. Who could ever say that he or she feels good enough in every area of his or her life? Feeling "good enough" is never the answer to lasting happiness. As soon as we feel good enough in one area, there are ten others where we feel insufficient or inadequate.

When we believe we should be better than we are, we become self-focused, self-centered, and self-absorbed. This leads to anxiety and compulsion, not joy and peace. In later chapters, we'll learn how to accept our not being good enough so we can learn to be happier without having to be perfect.

"I deserve more than I have, and more _____ means more happiness"

All of us have desires, longings, and wants. Much of the time these longings are legitimate, and there is nothing inherently sinful about them. In the introduction I shared about Francine who wanted a loving husband. She desired a better than average marriage. She wasn't asking for too much.

Rhonda had different longings. She wanted more power, more impact, and more purpose in her life. These also are good desires. The problem is when they switch from desires to demands, from longings to expectations. Then whatever we get will never be enough because we deserve more. The story line becomes, *It's all about me and all for me.* When our legitimate hopes, dreams, or desires move into the category of expectations, they escalate into demands—things we feel entitled to or deserving of. And when the demands aren't met, we can feel quite miserable.

Janet had many expectations and demands of others that were unhealthy and unrealistic. Again, most of them included the words *should* or *ought*. For example, Janet believed that her mother *should* be a better grandmother. Her friends *ought* to care more about her needs and feelings than they did. Since she continued to live her internal story as if she were both the main character and the most important one, she felt entitled to other people's attention and believed they should put her at the top of their priority list. Her needs, her rights, her wants, and her feelings should come first. Janet often told herself, *If they really loved me, they would care more about my needs and my feelings*. Therefore, when others failed to meet her expectations, she not only felt hurt and angry, she felt unloved.

Janet didn't just *desire* her mother to be more attentive and interested in her children, she *expected* her to be that way. You might argue, What's wrong with expecting your mother to be a good grandmother and to show interest and love for her grandchildren? Nothing's wrong with it—except it didn't line up with the way things really were. Janet's mother was not that kind of grandmother, and as long as Janet kept expecting she should be, Janet would continue to get hurt and disappointed.

The truth is, no one ever gets everything in life that he or she wants or desires. When we live as if we deserve people's love and attention all of the time, then we're not living in reality. Instead of learning how to handle in a mature way the inevitable disappointment of not getting all that we want, we stay miserable.

In addition to our own internal unrealistic expectations, we also live in a culture that encourages people to demand their rights and to feel entitled. After all, we're worth it! Because of this mind-set, people sometimes make terrible choices. They tell themselves they have the right to be happy and to pursue whatever it takes to be happy, even at the expense of others. I recall a woman I counseled telling me this very thing. She had fallen in love with her boss at work. She was a Christian, yet she believed God wanted her to be happy, and therefore he wouldn't want her to stay married if she found her true love elsewhere. Despite my fervent warnings to think more carefully, she chose to end her marriage in order to get what she wanted.

When we are the main character of our story line and it is all about us, then we justify pursuing what we think makes us happy, even if it makes those around us (like this woman's husband and three children) very unhappy. But we will never find true happiness at the expense of others. That will lead only to more heartache.

Whether our expectations are unrealistic, unhealthy, or just unmet, we become unhappy when we believe we're entitled to have more than we have. Instead of feeling thankful for what we do have, we grumble and complain about what we don't. The apostle Paul told us that he had discovered the secret of being content, whether he had a lot or a little (Philippians 4:11-12). The secret is surrendering to God's plan— not getting all your needs, wants, desires, or expectations fulfilled.

"Life should be easy and fair"

When we pine for an easy life, we forfeit a fulfilling life. We become bored and apathetic, not happy. Author Gary Haugen tells a story of going on a trip but missing the adventure. During a camping and hiking vacation to Mount Rainier with his father and brothers, his dad wanted them all to climb the rock formation heading to the summit. Gary felt afraid and asked his father to allow him to stay behind at the visitor's center where he could watch the videos and read about the wildlife and history of the mountain. After much pleading, his father finally relented. Here's the rest of Gary's story:

> The visitor's center was warm and comfortable, with lots of interesting things to watch and read. I devoured the information and explored every corner, and judging by the crowd, it was clearly the place to be. As the afternoon stretched on, however, the massive visitor's center started to feel awfully small. The warm air felt stuffy, and the stuffed wild animals started to seem just—dead. The inspiring loop videos about extraordinary people who climbed the moun- tain weren't as interesting the sixth and seventh times, and

they made me wish I could be one of those actually climb-
ing the mountain instead of reading about it. I felt bored,
sleepy and small—and I missed my dad. I was totally stuck.
Totally safe—but totally stuck.

After the longest afternoon of my ten-year-old life, Dad
and my brothers returned flushed with their triumph. Their
faces were wet from the snow; they were famished, dehy-
drated and nursing scrapes from the rocks and ice, but on
the long drive home they had something else. They had
stories and an unforgettable day with their dad on a great
mountain. I, of course, revealed nothing, insisting that it
was my favorite day of the whole vacation.

Truth be told—I went on the trip and missed the adventure.[1]

When Jesus tells us that he has come to give us an abundant life, he
doesn't mean a safe and comfortable life, but a meaningful one. He
calls us to a purpose beyond pleasing ourselves.

As we've already seen, Janet expected life to be easy and fair. She
seemed mentally, emotionally, and spiritually unprepared for life's ordinary bumps and hurdles. Yet Jesus clearly tells us, "In this world you
will have trouble. But take heart! I have overcome the world" (John
16:33). Jesus warns us that life isn't easy or fair, and he tells us this so
that we can experience peace and find courage in the midst of life's
hardships.

How? You'll find some specific tools in later chapters, but it starts by
seeing things as they really are. Jesus tells us that if our eye is healthy,
our whole body will be full of light (Matthew 6:22). Happiness, joy,
peace, and an internal sense of well-being are never found in having an
easy life or in a life full of possessions, power, or popularity. We only
have to look at some of the Hollywood celebrities gracing the news
these days to see individuals living an easy life. On the fairness quo-
tient, they have the deck stacked in their favor. They have most of the
things we tell ourselves we need to be happy. They are thin, beautiful,

rich, popular, powerful, and have lots of possessions. Yet many of them appear purposeless and empty and actually look quite unhappy. These men and women may have pleasure, power, prosperity, and popularity, but they do not have happiness. Never confuse those things with a genuine inner sense of joy, peace, and well-being.

In fact, it is often when life is easy and good, plentiful and prosperous, that God warns us we are in the most danger of losing sight of what brings our soul true delight. When the Israelites were entering the Promised Land, God warned them,

> When the LORD your God brings you into the land he swore to your fathers, to Abraham, Isaac and Jacob, to give you—a land with large, flourishing cities you did not build, houses filled with all kinds of good things you did not provide, wells you did not dig, and vineyards you did not plant—then when you eat and are satisfied, be careful that you do not forget the LORD, who brought you out of Egypt, out of the land of slavery (Deuteronomy 6:10-12).

The Adaptation Principle

If we want to increase our capacity for genuine inner happiness, we must begin to debunk our belief that having more _____, or changes in our life circumstances, will make us significantly happier than we already are. The problem with this thinking is that it feels true. Losing weight, or getting a new job, home, or husband does make us feel happier for a time, but it's only a temporary fix. After we get what we want, our mind naturally moves on to the next thing that is wrong, or what we want, or what we believe will make us happy.

When Janet finally found a new job that she liked and that paid well, she felt much better. But her newfound happiness lasted about two weeks. Then she was right back where she had been—unhappy with her life, even though she liked her new job. Psychologists have called this the *adaptation principle*. Over time, we become accustomed to or get used to our new life situation, whether it is better or worse, and eventually return to our normal happiness range.[2]

• • • • • • • **I'll Be Happy Forever, Mom!** • • • • • • •

I remember my son, Ryan, endlessly nagging me for a special toy. He was convinced that if only he had this one gadget, life would be good. He was so persuasive, I believed him. Eager to make him happy, I bought him the toy. He was thrilled. But three days later, I saw it lying under his bed. Now he was pleading for a new plaything he needed to be happy. As adults, often we're not any different.

• •

The writer of Ecclesiastes discovered this truth much earlier than the psychologists did. This book is written by a king who had an easy life. Most believe it was written by King Solomon, King David's son with Bathsheba. Solomon had everything he wanted and enjoyed the things our culture promotes as giving us a satisfying life. He had enormous power, whatever pleasure his heart desired, plenty of possessions, a productive life, popularity, and over 700 wives and 300 concubines. Yet in the end, when he looked over everything in his life, it felt empty. Power, possessions, popularity, and prosperity weren't enough to bring him true happiness.

The king discovered, as we all must if we want to find authentic happiness, that he had wrongly depended on something other than God to give him what only God could give.

Dismantling Our Story Line

To begin the process of learning *how* to be a happier person, we must see the deception of our internal story line and replace it with the truth. Most of us feel powerless to do this without some outside help. God already knows our weaknesses, and so what he often does to free us of our illusions and delusions is allow disappointment, pain, and suffering into our lives. This gives us the chance to wake up and see what matters most.

Recently, I was talking with Beth, who, like Francine, has been chronically disappointed and unhappy in her marriage. Her expectations for a loving and intimate relationship with her husband have never been met, and her years of heartache over such disappointment were laced with resentment and anger. But through some unexpected health problems, she has begun to wake up to her life and to a deeper walk with God. As a result, she's appreciating the smaller things and noticing what's good in her marriage instead of what's wrong. She has learned to let go of her expectations without deadening her desires for a better relationship. And that's an important distinction. It's not that we don't desire certain things, but we don't *demand* them anymore!

"It hasn't been easy finding this path of joy and contentment," Beth said. "I can easily slip back into my old resentment and depression. This new road feels as thin as a thread's width. But I want to learn to stay on it."

Jesus tells us that the road that leads to life is narrow (Matthew 7:14). I don't think he is referring merely to eternal life; he's speaking about the abundant life. The king in Ecclesiastes pursued what he thought was the abundant life in all of his accomplishments, power, possessions, and pleasures. But through the disappointment of success,[3] he realized that even those wonderful things didn't offer him all he thought they would. He left these final words for us so we might glean understanding into what brings the heart true joy:

> Light is sweet; how pleasant to see a new day dawning.
> When people live to be very old, let them rejoice in every day of life. But let them also remember there will be many dark days. Everything still to come is meaningless.
> Young people, it is wonderful to be young! Enjoy every minute of it. Do everything you want to do; take it all in.

But remember that you must give an account to God for everything you do. So refuse to worry, and keep your body healthy. But remember that youth, with a whole life before you, is meaningless.

Don't let the excitement of youth cause you to forget your Creator. Honor him in your youth before you grow old and say, "Life is not pleasant anymore." Remember him before the light of the sun, moon, and stars is dim to your old eyes, and rain clouds continually darken your sky...

Yes, remember your Creator now while you are young, before the silver cord of life snaps and the golden bowl is broken. Don't wait until the water jar is smashed at the spring and the pulley is broken at the well. For then the dust will return to the earth, and the spirit will return to God who gave it (Ecclesiastes 11:7-10; 12:1,2,6,7 NLT)

The book of Ecclesiastes teaches us a powerful lesson. We will always be disappointed with life (or others) when we ask it to do something it wasn't designed to do. If we can learn to appreciate our life, our marriage, our job, or our family for what they are, then we can experience joy, wonder, and gratitude more readily.

Through Janet's disappointment with herself, other people, and life, she began to ask some important questions as well as gain some new insights that led her to see Christ, herself, and her life through a new lens. She finally began to grasp that it was her expectations that were causing much of her pain. She realized that when she expected so much from others, life, or even herself, then even the good things she did have or receive, were never good enough. As she surrendered her internal story line, Janet was surprised to discover some peace and happiness even in the midst of painful situations.

The psalmist also felt sad and perplexed over life's disappointments. But he came to understand through his suffering, that he needed to put his hope in God, not in other things (Psalm 42). Jesus loves us too much to leave us thinking or believing that a rich and meaningful life is found in anything other than loving and serving him. He tells us that where our treasure is, there our heart will be also (Matthew 6:21). Another way of saying this is, where our pleasure is, our treasure is also.

§

Jesus has come to set the captives free. Whether we realize it or not, many of us are captive to the lie that something other than God will bring us happiness and fulfill our longings. When we put our hope in or expect something or someone other than him to fill us and make us happy, he will surely frustrate us. But he doesn't do it to punish us. He does it to rescue us from our disordered attachments and delusions, and from ourselves. God promises to meet our needs—but what we feel we need, and what we truly need, may be very different.

Our disappointments and sorrows in life are gifts given to help us see things correctly. C.S. Lewis writes, "God whispers to us in our pleasures, speaks to us in our conscience, but shouts in our pains; it is His megaphone to rouse a deaf world."[4] Disappointment can lead us out of illusion and into truth and reality. Sorrow teaches us to let go of our attachments to false or lesser things and to seek after God. True prosperity is never acquired through worldly accomplishments or possessions, but rather through the awareness and ability to live in God's loving presence.

Peter tells us that suffering teaches us to be done with sin and to live for God's purposes rather than our own pleasures and evil desires (1 Peter 4:1-5). Why? Because suffering helps us surrender our illusions, desires, and expectations of what life *should* be so we're freed to live as God designed us to be (1 Peter 1:6).

Can you begin to let go by surrendering these lies to God, trusting him that he knows what you need to be happy? If you can't just yet, don't despair. He will help you. He wants to give you a new script to help you live a new story—a story that will bring more peace, more joy, more love, and more hope to your life.

1. How did you relate to Janet? Have you considered that some of your unhappiness may come from unmet expectations of God, others, or life?

2. If you haven't already, fill in the blanks: "If only I had more _____ or a better _____, I'd be happy." Recall a time when you got what you wanted. How long did your happiness last?

3. What do you think of this observation: "Expectations are longings and desires that have become demands"? What are your demands of God, others, or yourself?

4. German philosopher Arthur Schopenhauer stated,

    All striving springs from want or deficiency, from dissatisfaction with one's condition, and is therefore suffering so long as it is not satisfied. No satisfaction, however, is lasting; on the contrary, it is always merely the starting point of fresh striving.[5]

    How have you experienced this in your own life?

5. Which core lie do you struggle with? How has it affected your happiness levels?

  • I ought to be more than I am
  • I deserve to have more than God gave me
  • Life should be fair

6. Reflect on the author's statement, "When we believe we should be better than we are, we become self-focused, self-centered, and self-absorbed. This leads to anxiety and compulsion, not joy and peace." How have you found this to be true in your own life?

7. Read Psalm 73:12-14. Listen to Asaph's unspoken expectations of God as he surveyed his life and what was going on around him. Why did he feel he deserved better?

8. Discuss the difference between acknowledging the truth and emotionally accepting it. (For example, *I know I'm in a difficult marriage, but I'm not okay with it.*) Next, review each core lie:

  • I ought to be more than I am
  • I deserve to have more than God gave me
  • Life should be fair

In what ways do you acknowledge the truth throughout this chapter, but still resist emotionally accepting it? How does your refusal to emotionally embrace God's truth contribute to your unhappiness?

9. Read Acts 14:15. How has disappointment and suffering helped you turn from vain things and turn toward God?

10. Read Psalm 63. What steps can you take to be more satisfied with God and less hungry for other things?

11. Jesus came to set the captives free. How have you been trapped in your stories and scripts? What do you need to surrender in order to experience greater happiness in your life?

CHAPTER 2

Elephants Out of Control

*Nothing changes if nothing changes, and if I keep doing
what I've always done, I'll keep getting what I've always
got, and will keep feeling what I've always felt.*

UNKNOWN

*True realism consists in revealing the surprising things which
habit keeps covered and prevents us from seeing.*

JEAN COCTEAU

WHEN I WAS IN CAMBODIA, I had the opportunity to ride an elephant. This
was not a trained circus elephant, but an authentic jungle elephant,
and we were going for a ride through a real—not Disneyland-type—
jungle. As I sat inside a small wicker basket fastened to the elephant
by a thin and fraying rope, I started to worry over whether this was
a smart idea. (Remember, I am a pessimist and have worst-case-
scenario disease.)

Our travel group consisted of nine women, though not everyone
chose to participate in the ride. Those of us who had, bravely joked that
trotting through the Cambodian thickets on the back of an elephant
would be a true adventure. We were all busy snapping pictures of each
other, when all of a sudden my elephant decided he wanted to snack
on a few choice leaves off the trail. Off he went, crashing through tree

limbs and branches as I clung to the sides of the basket ducking inside to keep myself from getting battered by brush.

The elephant's owner, who was straddled across the animal's neck, furiously whacked him on the sides of his head with a wooden axe, but this elephant wasn't listening. He had a mind of his own. His appetite ruled him, not his owner. Thankfully, after he finished munching his leaves, he reluctantly returned to the trail, and we got back to base, safe and sound.

Sometimes our lives can feel like elephant and rider.[1] One part of us is charging ahead, doing things we know aren't good for us, like overeating, watching pornography, having fits of rage, worrying excessively, or having pity parties. All the while, the other part of us feels as helpless as the elephant's owner was powerless to stop his beast from bolting off the trail. We say we want to be ruled by Christ's love and produce the fruit of his spirit, but other forces, outside our own will and often outside even our own awareness, are at work. Like the apostle Paul, we cry out, "In my mind I really want to obey God's law, but because of my sinful nature I am a slave to sin" (Romans 7:25 NLT).

Why We Are the Way We Are

The Bible describes the human heart as deep, incredibly complex, and masterfully self-deceptive. And much of what goes on within our heart is totally outside our own awareness (see Psalm 139:23-24).

Only God can plumb our hearts and know us fully (Jeremiah 17:9). The Scriptures are clear about this much: Without Christ, we are in bondage, and our heart is automatically ruled by our fleshly and sinful cravings (see Romans 8). Even those of us who are in Christ often still feel trapped and powerless against our fleshly appetites, emotional upsets, and negative and oppressive thoughts.

Why is this? One of the main reasons is that we are habitual creatures and are ruled by our sinful or addictive habits, even when we don't want to be. Every human being, from the moment of birth, is being shaped as to who and what kind of person he or she will be. We are shaped by a number of factors. How we are treated and what we are taught by our parents, society, culture, school, friends, church—all of these greatly influence us. Day after day, week after week, month after month, and year after year, this formation process occurs.

It is not only what happens to us, however, that molds our character. We have a vital part to play in our own formation process. For example, a child can respond to her mother's *no* in a number of different ways. One child obeys, another challenges, still another collapses in a heap on the floor and screams to get her own way. These individual responses have nothing to do with the mother, but rather expose the child's heart. One response was obedient, the other rebellious, and the third one was manipulative.

As such positive and negative responses (that we all have) get repeated again and again in a person's life, they become internal patterns—habits of feeling, responding, thinking, being, and behaving—that determine in a large measure how we see ourselves, how we treat others, and how we navigate through the world. It's crucial we understand that who we are is not merely a result of what has happened to us or how people have treated us. Who we are and who we are becoming is formed as much, if not more, by our unique way of responding.

We can't change the past, nor can we always have control of what happens to us now. But the way we respond to people and to life shows us something about who we are. And our responses *will* affect our level of happiness. For example, do we automatically grumble and complain when we don't get what we want? Are we able to look for the good in a difficult or hard situation, or are we overwhelmed by it? When we're honest with ourselves, we have to admit that we have all developed some unhealthy habits in our external life and internal life. These lifestyle habits feel so natural and normal, we don't recognize that they are huge detriments to our well-being and happiness.

God promises that as new creations in Christ, we can change. We can learn to think new thoughts...even respond differently from the depths of our heart. This is what spiritual transformation is all about, and it leads us not only to a holier life, but to a happier one as well.

The apostle Paul tells us,

> Since you have heard about Jesus and have learned the truth that comes from him, throw off your old sinful nature and your former way of life, which is corrupted by lust and deception. Instead, let the Spirit renew your thoughts and attitudes. Put on your new nature, *created to be like God—truly righteous and holy* (Ephesians 4:21-24 NLT).

When Paul honestly shared his struggle with his divided self in Romans 7, he didn't leave us hopeless. He gave us the solution. It is Christ in us who not only sets us free but also gives us the power to say no to those old ways of life (Romans 7 and 8). Paul also gives us the process by which we learn, day by day, to put on Christ's nature. When we're willing, Jesus is reforming us, transforming us to be more and more like him.

For many of us, our everyday habits operate outside our awareness. Or when we see them, we justify them, rationalize them, minimize them, or excuse them, even when they lead to great heartache.

· · · · · · · · · **The Inside Comes First** · · · · · · · ·

Recently I received an e-mail from a woman who wrote, "My spouse is very negative. He's never happy with life and is constantly having a pity party for himself." She added, "He says he is a Christian, but he is unhappy and always complaining about what he doesn't have and what he cannot do."

This woman's husband is indeed unhappy, but it's important to note that it's not what is happening in his outer life that is his main problem. It's his internal attitude. It's the way he habitually thinks about life and responds when he doesn't get what he wants or feels he deserves. When nothing is right on the inside, then nothing can be right on the outside.

· ·

In our quest to learn how to be happier, it's important that we expose our destructive habit patterns, because much of our continued misery is a direct result of these habits. Only when we wake up and see something for what it really is, are we then able to challenge it and work toward changing it.

Let's examine some of the worst habits that lead to feeling miserable. See if you don't have at least one of them entrenched in your heart. In order to be happier, you will not only need to see it, you will also need to learn how to change it.

The Habits of Worry, Comparing, and Grumbling and Complaining

No one feels peaceful or thinks positively in every situation. Nor is this always beneficial. But what our mind and emotions habitually dwell on directly affects our mood, our attitude, and our behavior. Like the husband of the woman I mentioned, when we regularly brood on things that we don't like or that are wrong, painful, negative, or hurtful, we can't feel happy. It's impossible. The psalmist cried out, "My thoughts trouble me and I am distraught" (Psalm 55:2).

Constantly complaining, worrying, and comparing one's lot in life to others causes us to feel upset and unhappy. God has hardwired our thoughts to be influenced by our feelings, and our emotions are directly impacted by the thoughts we think. Dallas Willard, in his excellent book on spiritual formation, *Renovation of the Heart*, writes, "If we allow certain negative thoughts to obsess us, then their associated feelings can enslave and blind us—that is, take over our ability to think and perceive."[2]

Recently a friend of mine shared with me how she almost got caught in a spiral of negative thinking over something relatively minor, a spiral that could have ruined her entire day. The prior evening she had hosted a large party. As she was putting away the washed silverware she noticed a number of forks missing. She thought, *Who threw away my forks?* Immediately she felt annoyed.

As she went to search her garbage, she realized her husband already put the evening's trash out at the curb. The pickup was due any minute. Panicked and still in her bathrobe and slippers, she ran outside and started rooting through the trash bags looking for lost forks. The garbage collectors pulled up, but she made them wait while she looked. Thankfully she found her forks, but she felt humiliated.

You would think finding her silverware would have made her feel better, but instead, she found herself tempted to brood over how silly she must have looked to not only the garbagemen, but any neighbors who happened to be outside. In addition, she struggled to let go of her earlier aggravation about her guests tossing her good forks into the trash. However, once she became aware of what she was doing, she was able to let it go. She realized that it was an upsetting experience for the moment, but it didn't need to be one for the entire day.

Brooding, ruminating, and rehearsing the negative events in our life will make us miserable. Excessive worry about what people think, how people see us, or what might happen to us or those we care about result in the same misery. If we want to gain emotional and spiritual maturity, as well as greater happiness, we must learn to put our negative thoughts and emotions in their proper place.

The answer isn't to repress them or deny them. That only causes more unhappiness. Instead, allow them to be present. Examine them as to why you feel or think the way you do. We'll learn more about how to do this in the next chapters. For now, start listening for your stories and scripts. Once you recognize what you are telling yourself, you will often discover that in addition to the painful moment, you've made up a story that creates more suffering.

For example, Janet (from chapter 1) felt hurt when her friend didn't invite her to lunch. Her pain was real, and the fact that her friend hadn't invited her to lunch was true. However, Janet not only felt the pain of rejection in the moment, but then she also made up a story as to *why* her friend hadn't invited her over. She told herself it must be because she wasn't good enough or desirable enough. She imagined her friend having a wonderful lunch with all her more worthy friends. The made-up story created more suffering, and Janet spent the next week brooding over what was wrong with her and how miserable her life was.

It's important that we grasp that, as powerful as our emotions and thoughts may be, they are not always statements of what is ultimately real or true, good or right. In fact, it is when we are in the grip of our strongest emotions and thoughts that we are usually blindest to those things. Who hasn't in a fit of anger felt totally justified telling someone off, and then later when you could think more clearly, deeply regretted it?

Jesus tells us, "Don't let your heart be troubled. Trust in God, and trust also in me" (John 14:1 NLT). This implies that we ought to have some measure of control over our emotions, and that trusting God will help that process. But many of us feel as powerless to stop our negative thoughts or feelings as the elephant's owner was to stop his elephant from charging off into the jungle.

The first step in gaining some control over our negative states is to recognize our part. It is not just what happens to us that causes our strong emotions, but what we tell ourselves about what is happening to us. In the next chapter I will give you some specific tools for understanding and moving past your negative thoughts and strong emotions so that you are no longer enslaved by them. However, it's important to remember that nothing will be right on the outside of our life when things are not right on the inside.

The Habit of Busyness

Today people thrive on busyness. We are almost proud of it, and we feel lazy if our schedule isn't crammed full of tasks or activities. We fail to recognize how the habit of busyness robs us of happiness. We not only clutter our lives with too much stuff and with negative emotions, we pack them full of activity. Why has our *doing* overwhelmed our *being?*

Let's examine three underlying reasons for habitual busyness.

Cultural Pressures

We live in a world that defines a person's value and worth by his or her productivity and efficiency. How much we get done and how well we can do it are the benchmarks of a good day or professional success. The more efficiently we produce, the better we feel. The downside, however, is that continued good feelings depend on keeping up the momentum of doing more. This doesn't come without a cost. What is sacrificed in the whirlwind of too much doing is often our personhood, as well as our relationships with others.

God defines personhood and success very differently than our culture does. Jesus warns, "What good will it be for a man if he gains the whole world, yet forfeits his soul?" (Matthew 16:26). Thomas à Kempis writes in his classic *Imitation of Christ,* "Blessed are the ears that catch the pulses of the divine whisper and give no heed to the whisperings of this world."[3] From Christ's perspective, success isn't measured by how much we do, how much we earn, or how much we have, but by how well we love and what kind of person we're becoming in the midst of life's activities.

As Christians, we readily acknowledge the truth of God's Word, but in our daily lives many of us still fall prey to prioritizing productivity over building relationships and growing in godly character. How can we detect when we've slipped into this cultural mind-set? One way is to pay attention to what gets sacrificed or put on the back burner when time is crunched. Is it your doing or your being?

When my children were young, I chose not to work outside the home so I would have plenty of quality time to spend with them during their formative years. But even there I found myself bowing down to the idol of productivity and efficiency, impatiently yelling at my children when their needs or demands disrupted what I wanted to get done for the day. What that showed me was that getting things done was more important to me than growing in patience and practicing gentleness with my children.

I still find doing easier than being. Last year I attended a silent retreat. (A silent retreat is where you go to a retreat center and don't talk for the entire weekend, in order to make space for God.) I had attended one before, but never succeeded in being totally silent (never go on a silent retreat with your best friend). This time my spiritual director added an additional challenge. He told me he didn't want me to read anything while there except my Bible, and to do even that sparingly. *What?* Since I wasn't going to be talking, I had brought a suitcase full of good books on spiritual things. Now what would I *do* with myself? It was too cold to go outside and walk for any length of time. The first night I ended up going to bed at 8 PM. There wasn't anything else to do. I must have been more tired than I thought, because I slept through breakfast. Saturday crept by. By lunchtime, I had prayed everything I knew to pray, and I started to feel anxious. What was I going to do now? No distractions. No books. No talking. Nothing but God and me and the deadening silence.

I was strongly reminded throughout that weekend, "Be still, and know that I am God" (Psalm 46:10). My value and worth is not determined by my activity level or what I produce. Toward Sunday afternoon, God reminded me over and over again I didn't *need* to do anything right then. I could just sit and enjoy him. I don't think I'd ever done that before. When I returned home, my unopened suitcase was still full of unread books but my heart was filled with a peacefulness and rest I had not had for a long while.

People Pressures

A second reason many people do too much is that they believe their happiness depends upon receiving the approval and acceptance of others. People pleasers can't bear the idea that someone might be disappointed or unhappy with them in any way. As a result, they frantically do the things they believe they must do in order for others to be pleased with them, to accept them, to approve of them, or to need them. They are terrified of rejection or disapproval, and they bend over backward so they won't be abandoned, unneeded, or disliked.

Sandra rushed into her counseling session ten minutes late. Apologizing profusely she moaned, "Sorry I'm late. There's never enough time in the day to get everything I need to get done. I always feel like I'm rushing to get to the next thing. Is it ever going to stop?"

Sandra's tardiness for her counseling session was a regular pattern. She was so busy tending to everyone else's agenda, she often lost track of time. She rarely made her own needs a priority, and frequently she sacrificed herself not only to meet another's needs, but also to satisfy many of their wants.

When I asked Sandra to look at why she always put herself last, she said, "God wants us to love others and put ourselves last." When pressed further, she said she felt selfish if she used her time for herself, and she believed she should never say *no* to anyone if she could possibly say *yes*.

I took Sandra to Mark 1:29-38, where Jesus recognized his human limitations and took time out for both sleep and prayer. When Jesus decided to leave Peter's house and go to nearby villages to preach, he also left many people unhealed, disappointed, and perhaps even angry with him. Jesus knew he could not do it all. He didn't try to or feel guilty over it. He did only what his Father told him to. He was not dependent on what others thought of him but only on what his Father thought of him. The Scriptures encourage us to do likewise (Galatians 1:10).

If you want to break free from your people-pleasing compulsions, you must put an axe to the root of your problem, which is the fear of man and your own inner sense of unworthiness. Until you do that, you will be not be successful in curtailing your chronic busyness. In a moment of anger or exhaustion you may stop for a bit, but soon the cycle starts up again and your desire to please people and win their approval wins over your desire to take better care of yourself or even to please God.

Avoidance of Painful Internal Reality

For many of us busyness is an intentional way to avoid reality. We don't want to feel our feelings or look at what's wrong in our life. When we slow down, those realities creep in and make us feel awful. It's easier to stay busy.

Bob was a workaholic. Everyone said so, including Bob himself. But what made him drive himself to function like a machine instead of a person? He looked successful and powerful, but he was not happy, and no one knew that better than Bob himself. Yet he would not slow down. Why? He felt scared to examine his inner life and powerless to change. Work seemed like a good alternative, and at least there he was well-paid and got plenty of professional admiration and appreciation. It was a good anesthetic for the deeper pain he felt.

Busyness always dulls awareness, which is why it's one of Satan's favorite ploys. Whether he keeps us deceived into thinking that meaning and purpose is found in our productivity or people-pleasing tendencies, or blinds us to other problems brewing in our life through our nonstop lifestyles, he distracts us from God's perspective and eternal realities, which are the truest things there are. Busyness distracts us from the spiritual life. Busyness can even imitate the spiritual life.

Jesus has something to say to those of us who do too much:

> Are you tired? Worn out? Burned out on religion? Come to me. Get away with me and you'll recover your life. I'll show you how to take a real rest. Walk with me and work with me—watch how I do it. Learn the unforced rhythms of grace. I won't lay anything heavy or ill-fitting on you. Keep company with me and you'll learn to live freely and lightly (Matthew 11:28-30 MSG).

One of the skills in learning to be a happier person is awareness. We need to become aware of our bad habits that rob us of our peace, our joy, our hope, and our love. We need to be aware when our doing compromises our being, and understand that when we do that, we're out of balance. Doing *is* important, but only when it serves our being—the person we are or who God calls us to be. Last fall I sat out on my deck and watched the sun set over the hills. It was breathtaking. I couldn't remember the last time I had noticed it. God gently reminded me that he gives me this spectacular gift many evenings, but I'm usually too busy to notice.

• • • • • • • • • • **Take Time to Notice** • • • • • • • • • •

Emily, a character in Thornton Wilder's play *Our Town,* dies in childbirth. She begs to return and live just one more day of her life with her family. She is granted her wish, but is disappointed with the results. Before returning to the cemetery, she speaks with the Stage Manager:

"We don't have time to look at one another. (*Emily sobs.*) I didn't realize. So all that was going on and we never noticed...Do any human beings ever realize life while they live it—every, every minute?"

The Stage Manager pauses and says, "No. The saints and poets, maybe—they do some."[4]

• •

If we want to find happiness, let's follow the example of Mary of Bethany. She was so acutely aware of Jesus' presence that she sat quietly at his feet rather than busily scurrying about like her sister, Martha, did. Jesus said Mary had made the better choice.

The Habit of Being Self-Absorbed and Self-Centered

People who feel chronically unhappy must begin to recognize that they have become habitually self-absorbed and self-centered. When we're in that habit pattern, our thoughts are consumed with ourselves. What captures our attention is what we don't have, what people have done to us, what's wrong with us, what we want, what we need, and what we think and feel. Our life purpose revolves around improving ourselves, satisfying ourselves, explaining ourselves, protecting ourselves, justifying ourselves, defending ourselves, and making ourselves happy. Most of the time, we have no idea how self-absorbed we've become. But if you're an unhappy person, see if you recognize yourself among these specific habit patterns.

The Habit of Self-indulgence

We live in a culture that has endorsed self-indulgence as a way of attaining happiness. *If I want something, I should have it. If it feels good, I should do it.* And, because I deserve it and can't afford it, there's always credit. Consumer debt has skyrocketed because we want more—and we should have it because we're worth it.

People buy things they never use. Clutter control has become a multimillion-dollar business. Casual sex is acceptable, even among those who call themselves Christians.[5] Why not? It feels good. Americans are overweight because we overeat. People indulge their bad moods and bad tempers and then excuse themselves by saying, "That's just the way I am."

I'm not saying we should sell everything we have and live a simple life. (Although that idea has gained more attention recently as many people have discovered that instead of owning things, they now own us.) What I am saying is that it's normal for people to have desires and longings, and it feels good to get something we want—but we must also understand this important truth. So I'll repeat it again: No matter what we get, it will never be enough. As soon as one longing or desire is satisfied, three more will replace it.

The difficulty with challenging indulgence as a way of life is that it does feel good to indulge, even if only temporarily. That's why we do it. We don't want to stop, because once we stop, the pleasure ends. Those who become addicted to a substance such as alcohol, drugs, or chocolate or an activity such as gambling, shopping, or pornography do it because it initially feels good. The problem is, the feeling doesn't last. It requires more, and more, and more. What started as pleasure eventually becomes bondage (2 Peter 2:19). When we are ruled by our appetites and senses, we are slaves. Freedom isn't license to do anything we want. Freedom is the power to say no to what we want, for the sake of a higher good or goal.

To break free from the bondage of self-indulgence, we need to experience the pleasure of saying *no* through practicing the discipline of restraint. (More about this in chapter 8.) Recently one of my clients experienced this pleasure. She's been battling overeating for years and wanted to pig out. She felt hungry for some chocolate and found herself making excuses and rationalizing in order to say *yes* to her craving. But then she caught herself and said *no*. In that moment, she felt deprived. But she stayed with that feeling. Instead of gorging herself, she went to bed. She woke up feeling good. That surprised her. She had experienced the pleasure of saying *no,* and it lasted throughout the next day.

Former addicts know that it feels much better to be able to say *no* than to feel enslaved to one's *yes*. Next time you want to give into something, say *no* to yourself. This may be very difficult for those with a weak will. But God wants to strengthen our self-control muscle, and we exercise it by saying *no* to ourselves. Part of the good news of the gospel is that Christ has freed us from our inability to say *no* to temptation. For those of us who haven't learned to say *no* to ourselves very often, it will feel strange and even difficult at first. Practice saying *no;* refrain from self-indulgence, and give it some time to work. Then pay attention to how much happier you feel with yourself.

The Habit of Self-pity

Self-pity is a toxic form of self-indulgence we don't always recognize as destructive. Sometimes we find it comforting; other times we feel it's warranted. Everyone falls into it from time to time. But if you're in the habit of feeling sorry for yourself, you will never feel happy. When we live out of the script that *we should be more than we are,* and that *we should have more than we have,* we will be chronically disappointed with ourselves and others and be dissatisfied with life.

Our self-pitying thoughts often revolve around our abilities, attributes, and assets, or the lack of these things, as well as what other people have done wrong to us. *Why me? What about me? Poor me,* and *What's wrong with me?* are our constant complaints. We feel gypped, deprived, and often quite angry. There is no joy or peace. Hope is in the form of *I hope this passes soon,* or *I hope things go my way before too long,* or *I hope things change.* Our hope doesn't rest on Christ but rather in the situation being different. When we're caught in self-pity, no one else's love ever feels good enough, and we are incapable of loving others. We are too engulfed in our own misery.

Healthy and happy people recognize when self-pity has gone on too long and work to yank themselves out of it. This requires a loving sternness toward the part of us that is feeling sorry for ourselves. Last summer, I fell into one of the biggest pity parties I've had in a long while. It lasted for about a half a day, and I not only made myself miserable, I made everyone around me unhappy as well. In hindsight, it was a trivial matter. But in the moment, I blew it up in my mind as a major offense. (Of course it didn't help that for several days I had been running on empty and was exhausted.)

The only one that can stop your pity party is you. For me to break free from my self-absorption, I had to say to myself, *Enough! It's not all about you!* And then I forced myself to get out of my bed and do something productive. That helped me take my mind off myself until the feeling passed—which it will if you allow it.

The Habit of Self-hatred

When we fail to live up to our own expectations, self-hatred can be the result. Please don't mistake self-hatred for godly sorrow or biblical repentance. (See Paul's teaching on the difference in 2 Corinthians 7:8-13.) Self-hatred doesn't lead us toward Christ; rather it turns us in on ourselves. It erodes our soul and spirit like acid on metal.

In the Bible, both Judas and Peter failed to live up to their own expectations of themselves when they betrayed Christ. But their responses to their failure were quite different (see Matthew 26 and 27). Judas, filled with self-hatred over betraying an innocent man, killed himself. Peter also was mortified by what he had done, especially since he had earlier told Jesus he'd never betray him. Peter had declared confidently that he'd even die for him. But when Peter saw himself truthfully, instead of turning in on himself in self-hatred, he turned toward Christ with sorrow and humility and repented. Self-hatred poisons our joy, steals our peace, and leaves us hopeless. The internal anguish is hellish. It is never of God.

How do we stop this habit? The only appropriate response to seeing our own failure or inadequacy is humility and repentance. Self-hatred is nothing more than wounded pride. We are disappointed that we are not more than we are. The truth is, we're not—and when we can accept that truth, we will have incredible freedom and peacefulness. Why? Because we know and rest in the good news that Jesus loves and accepts us in spite of who we are or what we have or have not done. From that place we can make peace with who we are and where we are—and then like Peter, with Christ's help, we can surrender to God so he can transform us into the person he made us to be.

Questions for
• • • • • •
Thought and Discussion

1. Have you ever felt like the elephant and its owner—that is, one part of you goes off and does something that another part of you doesn't want you to do or feel? When that's happened, how have you handled it?

2. Each of us has been influenced by a number of factors. Recall some of the positive shaping factors in your past. What about the negative ones?

3. The author writes, "We have a vital part to play in our own formation process." How have you seen your own role in shaping the person you are becoming? Are you happy with the kind of person you're becoming? Why or why not?

4. The chapter details three habit patterns that cause unhappiness. Do you agree or disagree with the author's observations?

   - Complaining, comparing, and worrying
   - Chronic busyness
   - Self-absorption, self-centeredness, and self-hatred

5. Read Philippians 2:14. What do you feel like when you're around someone who constantly complains or grumbles?

6. The author describes busyness as a habit that robs us of happiness. She gives three main causes for excessive busyness: cultural pressures, people pressures, or avoidance of a painful internal reality. Can you relate to any of these reasons?

7. In what ways have you been caught up in the habit of self-absorption? Identify the ways this habit has contributed to your unhappiness and what steps you can take to break it.

8. What is your understanding of the difference between godly sorrow and self-hatred? When you are disappointed or angry that you have failed to live up to your own expectations, how do you handle those emotions?

9. Read Philippians 2:13. How is God working in you to give you both the willingness and the ability to do what pleases him?

10. Pick one area that you now identify as a bad habit. What specific steps can you take this week to begin to break it?

CHAPTER 3

Stuck in the Pit

*Let's not forget that the little emotions are the great captains
of our lives and we obey them without realizing it.*

VINCENT VAN GOGH

*Feelings are, with few exceptions, good servants.
But they are disastrous masters.*

DALLAS WILLARD

A cheerful heart is good medicine.

PROVERBS 17:22

AS A CHRISTIAN COUNSELOR, I've not only worked with people who have
been stuck in the pit, I've also gotten stuck there myself, more than a
few times. Perhaps, like me, you know the truth that God loves you and
is for you, but sometimes you have a hard time feeling it. Our anxiety
robs us of peace and joy and our negative thinking steals our hope.

One of the reasons we don't feel happy is because we're stuck in the
mire of our toxic feelings and we don't know how to get out. Perhaps
we're afraid to try because if we fail and fall back in, it feels worse than
before. Others of us are so used to living in the pit, we can't imagine
anything else. In fact, it feels rather scary to step forward and make a
change. It's easier to live like we've always lived.

Let me be honest. There are no quick fixes or easy answers. But I do know if you learn to practice the things that I'm showing you, you will be able to diminish your toxic emotions and let go of your negativity sooner—so you can feel happier. In this chapter I want to give you some specific tools to help you break free from the toxic emotions that capture us so easily. It's not that we will never feel them, but we can learn how to understand them as well as let go of them as quickly as possible so we don't continue to get stuck in the pit.

Understanding Toxic Emotions and Negative Thoughts

In the previous chapters we've covered some of the reasons that we're unhappy. Now I want to give you some specific tools that will help you identify and release your toxic emotions and negative thoughts more quickly. You may not need to follow every step to understand or process your emotions, but each one will help you in specific ways. If one way doesn't work, try another. There is no perfect way to climb out of a negative mind-set or a toxic pit, but climb you must if you want to learn how to be a happier person.

Externalize Your Negative Thoughts and Feelings

One small change that can make a big difference is just the way you think about your feelings. Instead of saying to yourself (or someone else), *I'm depressed,* or *I'm angry,* say it this way: *I'm aware I'm feeling or thinking* _____. Try it right now. What happens when you say it in this new way? You become aware of another part of you that is now able to *decide* what you want to do with your feelings or thoughts.

Each one of us experiences hundreds if not thousands of different feelings and thoughts throughout our day. Some we pay attention to, others we don't. However, it's important that we not allow our emotions or even our thoughts to define who we are. We are much more than just our temporary feelings or fleeting thoughts. When you say *I'm angry* instead of *I'm aware I'm feeling angry,* you're likely to get stuck in your anger.

Simply changing your phrasing indicates a powerful shift. Now you have your *feelings,* instead of your feelings having *you.* Our feelings are not who we are—they are just our feelings. And sometimes we hang on to them much longer than we need to. Creating this little bit of space empowers us to become aware of a larger self that can help the other part of us that is caught in the negative spin of emotional pain.

Accept Your Emotions with Compassion, Not Self-hatred or Condemnation

Once we become aware of our negative thoughts or feelings we often try to suppress them because we don't like having them. Other times we acknowledge they are there but feel guilty or shamed because of them. The result is that now our original emotions are compounded with additional toxic feelings and negative thoughts.

For example, Joanne was a caregiver for her elderly parents. Although she loved them dearly, she also began to feel resentful and angry that they demanded so much of her time. Her parents called her several times a day and seemed oblivious that she had her own life to live in addition to taking care of them. Once Joanne admitted her resentment, however, she was plagued with shame and guilt. These secondary emotions came because she told herself that she should be better than she was. (Remember those toxic scripts in chapter 1?) She believed that she must be selfish for feeling resentful and that she was a bad daughter because she didn't love taking care of her parents at all times.

As I worked with Joanne she came to understand that one part of her loved her parents and wanted to take care of their needs as they grew older. The other part of her wanted to live her own life. It wasn't either/or but both/and. Joanne also learned that these two desires often conflicted with each other. She needed to accept without self-hatred that sometimes she would have feelings of resentment or anger and that these feelings didn't define who she was, only how she felt at the moment. When she could look at them honestly, without adding shame and guilt, she could then ask herself some crucial questions in order to work on letting them go.

Ask Questions About Your Feelings

The psalmist asked himself, "Why are you downcast, O my soul?" (Psalm 42:5). Asking ourselves questions is a good place to start when we are aware that we are feeling unhappy. Ask your negative emotions, *Why are you here?* Pain usually has a reason. It is often trying to tell us something so we will take action.

If, like Joanne, you add shame and guilt to your original feelings, you can still say, *I'm aware I'm feeling shame and guilt because I'm feeling angry and resentful.* By this time I hope you can also say to yourself, *And it's because I'm aware that I'm still living with an old script that says I have to be better than I am. But I am discovering that the truth is, I'm not better than I am. I just am what I am. And right now, I am only one person, and I'm aware that I am feeling resentful and unhappy that I have to give so much of my time to take care of my parents, even though I love them very much.*

In addition, if we're feeling shame and guilt, it very well could be because we've done something wrong. These particular emotions function like the smoke alarms of our conscience. They warn us of danger and we better pay attention. As with Joanne's situation, sometimes it's nothing more than smoke from burnt toast, and you can quickly fan it away. Other times you must pay closer attention, because your conscience is warning you to stop what you are doing. When that happens, instead of staying stuck in your guilt or shame, however, ask yourself what you've learned from your mistake or sin. Rather than living with regret, make necessary changes and learn from it.

Here are some additional questions that will help you figure out what your feelings are trying to tell you. *Is there a problem I'm not facing? What purpose do my negative emotions serve right now?*

• • • • • • **Don't Ignore the Flashing Light** • • • • •

Our feelings often warn us that something's going wrong and we need to pay attention. When my daughter was a college student, her car's "check oil" light started flashing. But she ignored it, telling herself that as long as the car was still running, it must not be a big deal. The problem with her thinking was that by ignoring a small fix she created a much bigger problem. Her car's engine soon seized up, and adding oil was no longer going to fix the problem. She needed to have her engine replaced. In the same way, not facing problems brewing in our heart, our relationships, or our life doesn't make them go away. They just grow into larger problems.

• •

Joanne's resentment and anger were warning her that she was getting worn out. She was taking on a task that was too big for her, and if she didn't get some additional help or resources for her parents, soon she would be vulnerable to more serious problems. (Studies indicate that caregivers often suffer a diminished quality of life, stress-related illness, a loss of social, emotional, economic, and practical support. They also have high levels of depression, anxiety, and anger.[1])

Listen for Your Automatic Thoughts

God has hardwired our emotions and our thoughts to match. What our mind habitually dwells on will affect us emotionally and physically. When you think negative thoughts you will feel negative.

God instructs us to pay close attention to what we are telling ourselves. We are to take every thought captive to the obedience of Christ (2 Corinthians 10:5). We can't change our feelings directly, but we can go through the back door by addressing our thought life. God's Word tells us that we are transformed by the renewing of our mind (Romans 12:2). This doesn't mean we will change from being a negative thinker into a positive thinker. But it *does* mean we're to examine every thought, whether positive or negative, through the lens of Scripture to evaluate whether or not we are telling ourselves the truth.

Even when we know on one level that our thinking is not true, if we dwell on it long enough, it will affect us emotionally and physically. Who hasn't perched tensely on the edge of their seat while watching a scary movie? I was at the nail salon recently, and the dog movie *Marley and Me* was on their DVD player. The scene was the one where Marley is being put to sleep by the veterinarian. Although I knew it was just a movie, I still started crying (in the middle of getting my nails done), and I felt sad. Whatever holds our attention affects us emotionally. Our emotions are simply the chemical response to our thoughts. Negative emotions are triggered by negative thoughts.

Here is a tool I use in my counseling practice to help my clients identify their automatic thoughts. I encourage them to use it whenever they find themselves feeling emotions that they want to understand better. Start by naming the emotion. I'm aware I'm feeling _____. Write your emotions in column 3, and then backtrack and write down the situation that triggered them in column 1 and your automatic thoughts about the situation in column 2.

Here is an example of Joanne's chart.

Column 1: Situation	Column 2: Automatic Thoughts	Column 3: Feelings
My parents called me for the third time today.	Don't they realize I have a life? I shouldn't feel this way. They have been good to me. I'm a bad daughter.	Anger Resentment Guilt Shame

Once Joanne saw it was her thinking that was causing her emotions, not the situation, she felt empowered to counter some of her negative thoughts with the truth. She wasn't a bad daughter for feeling angry and resentful. It was just a sign she was getting worn out. It was also true her parents didn't realize she had a life of her own. Right now they were sick and elderly and wrapped up in their own needs. Joanne was the one who would have to make space to have her life without feeling guilty or feeling like a bad daughter.

Another client of mine, Charlene, became aware that she felt afraid to let go of her habitual negativity. Charting her feelings and thoughts in this way helped Charlene get in touch with what her emotions were telling her:

Column 1: Situation	Column 2: Thoughts	Column 3: Feelings
Leslie is coaching me to think differently.	This won't work. I can't do it like she wants me to. It will never be any different. If I fail I will be too sad. Even if I feel better for a while it won't last.	Hopelessness Anxiety

As Charlene completed her chart, it was obvious to her what was causing her hopeless and anxious feelings. It was her *stinkin' thinkin'*, the term psychologists often use about our negative and pessimistic thoughts. Charlene was aware of her feelings but wasn't as aware of her negative thoughts. They were as automatic and natural to her as breathing. Abraham Lincoln once said, "Most people are about as happy as they make up their minds to be." It's true. Happiness is first and foremost a mind-set.

If you recognize your own *stinkin' thinkin'*, instead of accepting every thought you have as true, challenge them. Ask yourself, *Is there another way of looking at the situation?* For example, Charlene could have seen my coaching efforts as something that God was giving her to help her break free from a lifelong habit of pessimism. Had she been able to switch to an alternate way of thinking, she might have been able to let go of her anxiety and hopeless feelings as well.

People have not only survived hellish experiences, like being in a concentration camp or having physical disabilities, but have even thrived in the midst of them because of the attitude of their minds. It's true that they don't like their situation, but somehow they are able to take a higher view and discover pockets of joy, peace, love, and hope in the midst of it. Other people, no matter how pleasant their outer circumstances are, can't grab hold of the blessings. Why? They are mentally focused on what they do not have or what is not right— and therefore they always feel dissatisfied.

If we want to grow in our skills in happy living as well as mature as Christians, we will need to take responsibility for our automatic thoughts, as well as every other thought we have, and with the Holy Spirit's help, challenge them with God's truth. We need to do this regularly and repeatedly, especially if we are prone to depression, guilt trips, shame, self-pity, and negative thinking. These habits have deep roots and are not easily eradicated. But you can learn to feel differently as you train your mind to see things as God sees them. More will be said about how to do that in later chapters, but for now understand that you can't change your feelings directly, but your feelings will change as you train your mind to think differently.

Don't Overanalyze

There is a vast difference in asking yourself some basic questions about your thoughts and feelings and getting caught in navel-gazing, in which you overthink why you are feeling or thinking a certain way. If you get trapped in that cycle, let go of trying to figure anything out for the time being and do something else. Clean your house, take a walk, enjoy nature, help a friend. Overthinking doesn't help you, it only makes you feel worse. Psychologist Sonja Lyubomirsky says,

> The evidence that overthinking is bad for you now is vast and overwhelming. If you are someone plagued by ruminations, you are unlikely to become happier before you can break that habit. I will go so far as to say if you are an overthinker, one

of the secrets to your happiness is the ability to allay obsessive overthinking, to reinterpret and redirect your negative thoughts into more neutral or optimistic ones. I have found that truly happy people have the capacity to distract and absorb themselves in activities that divert their energies and attention away from dark or anxious ruminations.[2]

Sometimes we just don't know why we feel a certain way. If you're spending too much time figuring it out, set a timer and give yourself a specific time limit, then stop. I've given you some tools for you to gain self-knowledge. When you become self-absorbed in figuring it all out or too self-conscious about seeing your weaknesses, you've gone overboard.

How to Let Go of Negative Emotions

Thus far we've talked about how to turn the corner in your mental attitude. That is the first step. You are examining your negative and untrue thoughts and starting to challenge them with God's Word. But I want to be real here. Sometimes no matter what you are telling yourself, there's another part of you that still feels hurt, anxious, down, crabby, or hopeless. Now what can you do to get yourself out of the pit?

Exercise Your Will

In order to let go of your negative feelings, you have to want to. This might sound like a no-brainer, but for some of us, actually letting go of our anger, depression, guilt, self-hatred, worry, or hurt isn't easy. We feel entitled, justified, or afraid to let them go. They have been our constant companions, our identity, our badge of honor. It's who we are and how we function.

When I asked one woman I counseled what she got out of hanging on to her resentment and fear, she paused. In a moment of clarity and personal honesty she replied, "I get to be the victim. If I let go of my resentment, then what?" When we consent to shed our toxic emotions, sometimes we're not exactly sure who we are or how to act anymore.

God has given us an incredible and powerful gift—and that is our ability to choose. We get to choose what we do and who we are becoming, moment by moment, day by day. Small choices, repeated over time, form habits, and habits shape our character. The good news is, it's never too late to begin to change our habit patterns. If you have been hanging on to your negative feelings as your rightful badge of identity, understand that it comes with a heavy price to pay. It's called *misery*. And you don't *have* to stay that way.

Take Care of Your Body

As Christians we forget that we are more than spiritual beings. We are also physical beings, and when our body is tired, hungry, sick, or hormonally challenged, our emotions and thoughts usually don't function well either.

Vicki, a bright and beautiful woman, came to see me about some depression. She had carefully crafted the perfect life but found herself feeling desperately unhappy. She had a large home, two beautiful children, a loving husband, and a good church, so what were her negative feelings telling her? Why were they here? Was there a problem she wasn't facing?

As we began to listen together to Vicki's inner dialogue, automatic thoughts, and desires, we began to uncover some of her own internal stories and scripts about how she thought her life should go. Even though her life circumstances were better than average, for Vicki they were still not good enough. She wasn't good enough. Her marriage wasn't good enough.

After working on her unrealistic expectations of herself, life, and others, Vicki was feeling much better. I didn't see her in a while until she came for a follow-up appointment. She was beaming. When I asked her what was different, she said, "I joined a gym and I've been working on eating healthier. Leslie, I can't believe what a difference those simple changes have made in my mood."

Many studies have confirmed the importance of diet and exercise to not only our physical health, but our emotional well-being. In a study conducted to measure the effectiveness of aerobic exercise on major depression, researchers found that regular and intense aerobic exercise was just as effective at treating major depression as antidepressant medication. An even more remarkable finding was that those individuals who continued their exercise regime after recovering from depression were far less likely to relapse than those who had taken antidepressant medication alone.[3]

When Elijah fell into the pit of despair and depression, God helped his body first through diet and rest. It was only after Elijah's body was nourished that God addressed his *stinkin' thinkin'* (1 Kings 19). Our physical body must take an active role if we want to get out of the pit of negative emotions and stay out. (One of my clients just told me that she had sent her youngster to bed for a nap. She was acting crabby and out of sorts, and no amount of reasoning would help. But a long nap did.)

When you're tense and anxious, learn how to take deep and slow breaths in order to calm yourself down. Curtail your intake of refined foods and white sugar. Relaxation training, sunshine, hugs, restful sleep, and even a healthy sex life are all important ingredients that help us let go of and dissipate our negative emotions. Who hasn't felt better after a good night's sleep, a brisk walk, sitting in the sun, or a warm embrace?

Address the Problem

Earlier we talked about identifying the problem. Once you do that, you also have to work toward a solution. When Joanne realized she was getting resentful over being a caretaker, as well as feeling guilty for feeling resentful, she begin to make some changes. She started with her own self-talk. She reminded herself that she was a good daughter and was willing to do many things to help her parents, but that she couldn't be a full-time caregiver. She still had her own life and responsibilities.

As Joanne accepted those realities, she planned a time to share with her parents that together they would need to make additional provisions for their care. She also had a meeting with her siblings and asked for more help. She felt empowered as she addressed the problem instead of being overwhelmed by it.

Ask yourself, *Is the problem I'm facing internal or external?* For Joanne it was both, as it often is. The internal problem she had to address was her own script that told her she was a bad daughter if she didn't do it all. The external problem was the reality of caring for her aging parents.

Other times the problem is primarily internal—one of our negative mind-set or toxic emotions. But until we take care of our physical needs by getting enough sleep, finding the proper medication, getting regular exercise, or making dietary changes, we stay stuck. Even if we get some relief temporarily, the negativity creeps back.

Talk with Someone to Get a Different or Larger Perspective

If you're having a difficult time seeing the forest for the trees, it's time for another perspective. Sometimes we just aren't able to see our way clear through the fog of our negative emotions. In Psalm 73, Asaph almost lost his way in the midst of his negative feelings about life. He could not understand why the good guys suffered and the bad guys got away with treachery. He despaired at the unfairness and injustice of life—until he entered into God's sanctuary where he saw things differently.

Jeremiah too despaired of life and was angry at God. He had lost his hope because he thought God was against him. When he remembered the truth, his hope was restored. Read through Lamentations 3 and listen to Jeremiah's automatic thoughts. Pay attention to how they impacted his mood. Suddenly, beginning in verse 21, there is a dramatic shift in his perspective. (It might not have been so sudden in Jeremiah's actual experience—it may have come more gradually.)

> Yet this I call to mind and therefore I have hope:
> Because of the LORD's great love we are not consumed,
>   for his compassions never fail.
> They are new every morning; great is your faithfulness.
> I said to myself, "The LORD is my portion; therefore I
> will wait for him" (Lamentations 3:21-24).

It was Jeremiah's change in perspective that impacted his feelings, not a change in his external circumstances. God's Word helps us see things differently. God also uses wise people (and books) to help us get a different perspective.

Distract Yourself (Switch Channels)

When I'm watching something disturbing on television, I switch channels and get my mind on something else. If all else fails and you are still finding yourself stuck in the midst of an emotional storm, it helps you to focus on something else for a while. For example, Debbie was furious and brokenhearted after learning of her husband's affair. Although they were working on rebuilding their relationship, she had real doubts as to whether their marriage would make it. All she could think about was her husband, Steve, with that other woman. Picturing them together sickened and enraged her. She did not know how to let her thoughts and feelings go, and at the moment could not get a different perspective.

Debbie looked at her thoughts as she wrote them down, and she found that most of them were true. Her husband had betrayed her. She wasn't sure they would make it as a couple, and the consequences of his affair fell not only on Steve, but on their entire family. How could she let her emotions go?

It wasn't time for Debbie to let them go entirely. They actually still served a purpose. Their intensity allowed her husband to see how deeply his sin had hurt her and their marriage. Had she been able to let go of her negative emotions without struggling, Steve might have minimized the seriousness of his sin. Debbie's emotional turmoil motivated her and Steve not to take his affair lightly and to not only look at Steve's reason for having the affair, but also to look for cracks in their marriage that might have contributed to his making that choice.

In the midst of still feeling rage and hurt, there were some things Debbie could do. She could watch a funny movie, go out with friends, take a long walk in a beautiful park, or groom her dog. She needed to take a break from her emotional intensity and distract herself. (In chapter 10 we'll also learn how to find the good in bad situations. Actively looking for the lessons learned or benefits received from our trials can actually strengthen us as people and contribute to an overall greater happiness level.)

When I was pregnant with our first child, my husband was diagnosed with cancer. I became overwhelmed with fear. My emotions weren't going anywhere, at least for the time being. But I did get some temporary relief from them by sleeping, taking care of my body, keeping busy playing board games with friends, doing cross-stitch, and distracting myself with other things.

Practice the Opposite

One of the things that can be very helpful in the moment of strong emotion is to choose to act out the opposite virtue. For example, when you're feeling jealous of another person's good fortune, write them a sincere letter congratulating them. When you're feeling impatient, take a slow deep breath and be extra kind. When you're feeling angry toward someone, determine to show mercy and compassion rather than anger.

Don't misunderstand me. I'm not saying that we should be hypocrites. Rather, this strategy goes back to not allowing our temporary feeling state to define who we are. Just because I feel angry at the moment doesn't mean I have to act that way. I feel lots of emotions throughout each day that I don't act upon. When I intentionally choose to behave in a way that's opposed to how I feel in the moment, I am applying a helpful antidote to an emotional poison. That's why Jesus commanded us to love our enemy and to do him good (Matthew 5:43-44). Acting the opposite doesn't mean we don't feel angry, it just means that we're not going to give in to our emotions by acting in an ugly way toward our enemy. In fact, in order to counter that ugly feeling, we *must* do him or her good.

One of the things I have intentionally done when I have negative feelings toward someone is pray for them. I don't pray that they would be struck down; I pray for their good. As I do that, the hatred or anger I feel often melts into compassion and mercy for them. We want to learn to act out of who we *are,* not what we feel. When we do that, our feelings will change.

Journal

Sometimes we just need to vomit out all our negative feelings. It feels better when we do so, but vomit belongs in the toilet and not on another person. Journaling is a good way to dump out negative emotions without feeling you have to be constructive about your words. It's also a very helpful way to clarify what is really bothering you. Sometimes our mind isn't quite able to put what's troubling us into words until we actually write it down and externalize it. Then you might find some things that are upsetting you that you didn't realize before. And you can look for your automatic thoughts so you can start making corrections or implement some of the other steps.

Prayer and Worship

Worship involves much more than singing hymns or praise choruses in church. In genuine worship, we bow ourselves before the lordship of God in our lives. We surrender to his will, even when our mind doesn't understand. We take our eyes off ourselves and our problems and focus them on God. The psalmist prayed, "When anxiety was great within me, your consolation brought joy to my soul" (Psalm 94:19).

The Bible tells a story of Hannah, a childless wife, who was grievously provoked by her husband's other wife, who had children. Hannah felt miserable. She could not eat and cried continuously. Distraught, she went to the temple and begged God to help her. Like Hannah, sometimes we find that we are so desperate for something from God that our entire welfare seems to rest on getting what we want. While she prayed, Hannah's anguish was so obvious that the priest, Eli, thought she must be intoxicated. Not so. She was praying out her great sadness and hurt. She told God what she felt and what she wanted, and surrendered all her desires and negative feelings and left them at his feet.

Afterwards, Eli the priest prayed also that God would grant Hannah her request. But the remarkable thing was that it was after Hannah's prayer, but before she was pregnant, that she stopped feeling sad (1 Samuel 1:18). God did bless Hannah with a son, who she dedicated to the Lord at a very young age. She realized that it was God and God alone who was the source of her joy, not her child. After she brought her son, Samuel, to the house of the Lord she prayed and praised God. She said, "My heart exults in the LORD; my strength is exalted in the LORD" (1 Samuel 2:1 ESV).

John Calvin says,

> Prayer has two parts; Petition and thanksgiving. Petitioning we lay before God the desire of our hearts, thus seeking from His goodness what serves His glory, and then what is useful to us.[4]

Practice Silence and Meditation

While speaking at a women's conference, an attendee told me that what helped her the most in her battle with depression was a self-imposed half hour of total silence each day. As a mother of six who homeschooled her children, she lived under a constant barrage of noise. Depression had plagued her for years, long before children, but having six kids in ten years took its toll on her body as well. Silence gave her body and mind time to recharge, and it made all the difference in this mother's mood.

In addition to silence, researchers worldwide have reported the positive benefits of a regular practice of meditation:

> An avalanche of studies has shown that meditation has multiple positive effects on a person's happiness and positive emotions, on physiology, stress, cognitive abilities, and physical health, as well as on other harder-to-assess attributes, like "self-actualization" and "moral maturity."[5]

The regular practice of meditation is stressed throughout the psalms. St. Francis de Sales said, "Half an hour's meditation each day is essential, except when you are busy. Then a full hour is needed." Psychologist Jonathan Haidt adds, "Meditation has been shown to help people stay calmer, less reactive to the ups and downs and petty provocations of life."[6]

- - - - - - - - - - - - **Smile** - - - - - - - - - - - - -

When all else fails, simply smile. That may sound silly, but in one study researchers asked students to hold a felt-tipped marker in their mouths. One group was instructed to grip the markers between their teeth, which simulated a smile, the other group between their lips, simulating a frown. The students had no idea of the purpose of this experiment. After they were done, they showed both groups some *Far Side* cartoons and asked them to evaluate how funny they were. The students in the smile group judged the cartoons more humorous than those in the frown group.[7]

Another study monitored bodily sensations during particular facial movements. The researchers said, "What we discovered is that the expression alone is sufficient to create marked changes in the autonomic nervous system. The face is an equal partner in the emotional processes."[8] God has amazingly wired our facial muscles to signal our brain to release chemicals in our body. Choose joy!

- -

❧

I hope you're beginning to realize that your happiness cannot be dependent upon everyone treating you the way you want. Else you will never be happy. Decide today, *I will no longer allow how others treat me, as well as my own negative feelings and thoughts, to dominate my life.*

Next, choose to pray and learn to trust God. This too becomes easier and more natural the more we do it. The apostle Paul specifically instructs us to *focus* our mind on more positive things. He is coaching God's people to pay more attention to what is good in their lives rather than rehearsing what's bad. He counsels those of us who feel trapped by negative mind-sets and emotions with these wise words: "Keep putting into practice all you learned and received from me—everything you heard from me and saw me doing. Then the God of peace will be with you" (Philippians 4:9 NLT).

In other words, Paul is telling us we need to build new habits and that these are only built through repeated practice. You will learn some additional ways to let go of bad thoughts and negative emotions in part 3, but start now. As you learn to do so, you will experience greater peace, more joy, and more happiness in your life as things gradually become right on the inside.

The habits we've covered in the last two chapters can be difficult to change because they are—well, habits. But God says we can break them as we become more aware and intentionally choose to do something different, one incident at a time, one decision at a time.

Later on, in chapters 10 and 11, we will learn how to *transform* negative situations and explore the benefits and blessings of practicing gratitude, both powerful antidotes to staying stuck in the pit of toxic emotions.

Let's now turn our attention to how our daily choices—including how we choose to handle our emotions—impact our internal well-being, for good or for bad.

Questions for
· · · · · ·
Thought and Discussion

1. Were you surprised by the author's assertion, "Our feelings and thoughts are not who we are, they are just our feelings and thoughts"? How have you allowed your negative feelings or thoughts to consume you?

2. Preacher and author Charles Spurgeon said,

   A troubled heart makes that which is bad worse. It magnifies, aggravates, caricatures, and misrepresents. If just an ordinary foe is in your way, a troubled heart makes him swell into a giant.[9]

   Read Proverbs 4:23. From this chapter, what specific steps can you begin to practice in order to guard your heart from being troubled?

3. Read Deuteronomy 7:17; 8:17-18; and 9:4-5. Pay attention to how God instructs the Israelites to think. Make a chart like you see on pages 62 and 63? What was the situation, what did God tell them to think, and what were the feelings he wanted them to have? What feelings might they have had if they had thought in a different way?

4. Why have you hung on to your emotions longer than necessary? Do you feel entitled? Afraid to let go or of them returning? What steps have you learned from this chapter that will help you let go faster?

5. Do you ignore your emotions, hoping the problem they reveal will go away? How has that habit created more problems and greater unhappiness in your life?

6. Read Proverbs 14:30. What are the physical consequences of good emotions?

7. What specific things have you learned you can do to help your body process your negative thoughts and emotions better? Pick one and begin to implement it this week. Pay attention to how it affects your emotional well-being.

8. Intentionally practice the opposite virtue and pay attention to how you feel. Show compassion and kindness when you feel irritated or angry, slow down when you're impatient and in a hurry, or do something for someone else when you feel you aren't getting enough. Remember, you have to exercise your will in order to oppose your emotional state in that moment.

9. What is the most helpful thing you've learned in this chapter? Commit to practicing it regularly in order to make it a part of your habit life.

CHAPTER 4

Recalculating

*Take care of the minutes, for the hours will take care of
themselves. This is the best path to gradual change.*

LORD CHESTERFIELD (AS TOLD TO HIS SON)

*You have brains in your head.
You have feet in your shoes.
You can steer yourself
Any direction you choose.*

DR. SEUSS

LAST YEAR I BOUGHT MY HUSBAND a GPS (global positioning system) for
Father's Day. He loves gadgets and had had his eye on one for some
time. I never thought I'd use it myself, because I am not good with
anything electronic. But then I had to travel out of town, rent a car,
and drive myself to several unfamiliar locations, so my husband gave
me a lesson in programming the system and off I went (with paper
maps in hand, just in case).

It took me a while to get used to Stella's voice (that's what we called
her), but before long, she became my new best friend. She told me
where to turn and how soon the turn was coming. And the absolute
best part was, she told me when I made a mistake. She never embarrassed me by pointing out my error—she gently said, "Recalculating."

It was her intent to get me to my location, and if I veered off in the wrong direction, she wanted to get me back on track as soon as possible so I would continue the course I had set for myself. The only catch was that I had to believe what she was telling me. And truth be told, sometimes I thought I knew a better route than she did.

In the same way, God provides specific instructions in the Bible (God's Positioning System) that tell us how to experience greater peace, authentic love, lasting hope, and inexpressible joy, in addition to how to live a meaningful life. We've already established that all of us instinctively head toward what we think or believe will make us happy and give us the good life we all crave. The problem we encounter along the way is we fail to believe that God's instructions will actually take us there. In addition, when we make wrong choices or poor decisions and end up miserable, we often continue to ignore his directions about how to turn around and recalculate in order to get back on track. We believe we know a better route.

Refusal to Recalculate

Recently I was driving with one of my friends and her children. Her oldest child, Tim, was not happy, and everyone in the car knew it. Earlier in the day, he had made a poor choice and didn't listen to his mom. As a result, he lost certain privileges for the next day. Tim felt bad about the punishment, but not bad enough to recalculate his behavior. He continued crying and complaining long after his mother warned him that more negative consequences would follow if he didn't stop.

It was interesting that Tim decided to continue in his misery rather than make different choices. He didn't seem to connect the dots that his suffering was the direct result of his own behavior. In his mind, it was not his fault but everyone else's fault. He blamed his mom for being hard-hearted. He made excuses and would not listen to her advice on how to rectify the situation. It reminded me of Israel's stubborn refusal to listen to God's correction throughout much of the Old Testament. For example, Jeremiah wrote,

> This is what the LORD says: "Stand at the crossroads and look; ask for the ancient paths, ask where the good way is, and walk in it, and you will find rest for your souls. But you said, 'We will not walk in it'" (Jeremiah 6:16).

Perhaps you are beginning to see that some of your misery is a result of the habitual ways you respond when you're disappointed or things don't go your way. Or you realize you've been doing something you thought would bring you life, but the results feel more like death. You want to learn where you can find genuine joy, experience inner peace, and have more hope and love in your life. But so far, you've not listened to God or to others who have tried to show you the way.

The Bible warns us that whatever a person sows, they reap (Galatians 6:7). This means that over time, when you sow good things in your life, you will usually reap the benefits of those efforts. On the other hand, if you sow weeds, don't expect roses.

In parts 2 and 3 we will learn the kinds of things we can sow into our lives that bring more joy, hope, love, and peace. For now, however, understand that pain and suffering can be a gift, when they cause us to recalculate. That's the purpose of consequences, to instruct more than punish. They teach us to choose differently faster so we don't continue to hurt ourselves. The heat of a hot stovetop creates pain when we put our hand on top of it. That pain warns us to STOP and move our hand away immediately. Without the pain, there would be no warning to pull your hand back before you got severely burned.

Pain and suffering aren't the antithesis of authentic happiness. If they lead us to take corrective action (whether externally in the way I live my life, or internally in the way I process my life), then they can truly be a blessing. When we refuse to learn from it, though, our suffering usually converts itself into long-term misery. Proverbs says, "He who is often reproved, yet stiffens his neck, will suddenly be broken beyond healing" (Proverbs 29:1 ESV).

Understanding the Decision-Making Process

There are many decisions we make throughout our day that we don't think much about, we just act. For example, we don't have to decide to breathe. We just breathe thousands of times a day and never give it a thought unless we're having trouble. When driving in familiar territory, we usually don't think about what road to take, where to turn, or even when to put our foot on the brakes when we're approaching a stop. We do these things automatically. (Like the habits we talked about in chapter 2.) In the early morning one part of me snuggles deep under the covers telling myself that it's too cold to get up, while another part of me already decided to get up and is flinging back the blanket and swinging my legs over the side of the bed.

As infants, we make all of our decisions simply by our body telling us what feels good and what feels bad. Our brains are hardwired to approach things that bring pleasure and avoid situations that bring pain. That's why curious children may get injured when exploring pleasurable objects like hot stoves, electrical outlets, and sharp knives. When they are not stopped, the pain they encounter teaches them to recalculate and not repeat that particular behavior again. However, human brains don't fully develop the capacity to weigh alternatives and make good judgments until adulthood and that explains why children and adolescents don't think about the negative or painful consequences of their choices before they make them. If it feels good, they approach again and again with gusto. That's one reason God gives them parents; to help them make good choices and train them in healthy habits.

Even as adults, however, we make many of our decisions using our automatic processes versus conscious choice. Professor and researcher Jonathan Haidt calls it our "like-o-meter" and says "its influence is subtle, but careful experiments show that you have a like-dislike reaction to everything you are experiencing, even if you're not aware of the experience."[1] For example we've all encountered someone with whom we just didn't click though we didn't know why. We just didn't like him or her.

Our emotional brain makes decisions based on what we like and don't like, as well as other sensations, hunches, intuitions, and gut feelings. It can save our life in a dangerous situation because it makes split second decisions without waiting for a consultation from our thinking brain before taking action.

For example, when you step on a tack, your pain tells you to immediately pick your foot up before your thinking brain even has a chance to tell it to do so. When in danger, our fight-or-flight response is activated. In many situations, our automatic response is a very good thing. At other times it gets us into trouble. Our emotions, hunches, and gut feelings aren't facts and don't always tell us the truth. That's why God also gives us a thinking brain which can weigh the pros and cons, look at situations from more than one angle, and understand that short-term pleasure may lead to long-term pain. When you make good decisions in the present moment, future moments often improve.

Psychologist Daniel Goleman, in his powerful book *Social Intelligence,* helps us grasp the importance of our decisions over time. He says, "The human brain is designed to change itself in response to accumulated experience."[2] When we've accumulated habit patterns that lead to emotional turmoil, negative processing, and internal misery, we can change them, but the way we do so is by learning to recalculate and make wiser choices, one decision at a time.

Making Better (Not Perfect) Choices

As we've seen, most of the decisions we make every day we make without thinking much about them. My husband coaches girls' volleyball. During a match, his athletes don't consciously think about executing good volleyball skills. Rather, in the heat of a game, they just do what they've learned. But when one of his athletes is in a rut, exhibiting poor serving or hitting techniques, she must start to be intentional about making a change; otherwise her body will do what it's always done, especially when under stress. The Cambodian elephant followed his tummy (emotional brain) rather than his owner (thinking brain), when yummy leaves were beckoning to him. Why would he have functioned any differently than he was used to just because he had a guest riding on his back?

Because we are habitual creatures, we too will do what we've always done (physically, mentally, emotionally, relationally, and spiritually) unless we stop, become aware, and intentionally choose differently. Over time, our new choices create healthier habits which can result in actual brain changes. To break bad habits and learn how to make better everyday decisions, start by taking these small steps.

Take Responsibility

One of the most important skills we must learn if we want to feel happier is how to take responsibility for our choices and recalculate. Otherwise we usually repeat the same mistakes again and again and, like Tim, usually blame others, bad luck, or God for our misery (Proverbs 19:3).

Here's one of my favorite poems that illustrates this path many of us find ourselves in.

Autobiography in Five Short Chapters

CHAPTER ONE

I walk down the street.
>There is a deep hole in the sidewalk.
>I fall in,
>I am lost…I am helpless.
>>It isn't my fault.
>It takes forever to find a way out.

CHAPTER TWO

I walk down the same street.
> There is a deep hole in the sidewalk.
> I pretend I don't see it.
> I fall in again.
I can't believe I am in this same place.
> But it isn't my fault.
It still takes a long time to get out.

CHAPTER THREE

I walk down the same street.
> There is a deep hole in the sidewalk
> I see it there.
> I still fall in…it's a habit…but,
> > My eyes are open.
> > I know where I am.
It is *my* fault.
I get out immediately.

CHAPTER FOUR

I walk down the same street.
> There's a deep hole in the sidewalk.
> I walk around it.

CHAPTER FIVE

I walk down another street.[3]

PORTIA NELSON

As this humorous poem illustrates, many of us initially see the painful consequences we're experiencing as something outside our control. We cry out "God, why did you allow this to happen to me?" with little awareness that we are the ones who have caused our own turmoil. If you're like me, you might hear yourself saying something like, "It's your fault I lost my temper." Or, "If only you wouldn't have done _____, then I wouldn't have reacted that way."

But try giving that excuse to the police officer who arrests you after you've smashed your car into the bumper of the driver who just cut you off. Like it or not, we are responsible for our choices, no matter who or what provokes us. We can't always control the situation we're in, nor can we control another person's behavior, but we must learn that we don't have to just react (emotional brain). God gives us the power to choose our response (thinking brain). The earlier we grasp this important truth and practice slowing down our knee-jerk reaction (the emotional brain) the better our life will go.

The difficulty people encounter in taking responsibility is that we get stuck arguing over who's at fault instead of looking for our part. The driver who recklessly cuts people off is clearly in the wrong. What we fail to notice is our own culpability. But, one might argue, "I was just driving, minding my own business, when he cut me off." That's true, but then what? What were your choices? Not everyone who is cut off by a reckless driver retaliates with rage. Some might mutter profanities; others might whisper prayers for that careless driver. Jesus says quite clearly that out of the overflow of your heart, *your* mouth speaks (see Luke 6:45).

In this case, what we can take responsibility for is that right now we are not able to handle being provoked or insulted without losing our temper. Now we have identified something to work on so that we can learn to handle provocative situations better in the future.

• • • • • • • • • • • **Donna's Script** • • • • • • • • • •

Donna felt chronically unhappy with herself because of her weight. She felt powerless over food and not only overate, but berated herself afterwards. It wasn't that Donna believed that being thin was the answer to all of her life's problems, but she did feel convicted that she should take better care of her body. Yet, Donna lived out of the script *I should be better than I am,* which kept her from taking responsibility for her poor food choices.

Donna would buy all kinds of snacks that she loved to eat. She told herself that she should be able to eat these foods responsibly and that she ought to have more self-control. But the truth was, she wasn't as capable in those areas as she thought she should be or wanted to be. Until Donna acknowledged and took responsibility for where she was, instead of beating herself up for failing to be where she wanted to be, she could not make better choices.

• •

Like the elephant and his owner, when we put ourselves too close to temptation, temptation will usually win out. We need to avoid temptation, not wrestle with it. Once Donna (see sidebar) understood that her body will always want to eat what her body is used to eating, she took responsibility and started to make better decisions. She stopped bringing tempting goodies into her home. Once she made that choice, it wasn't as easy for her to make poor food choices when she felt vulnerable.

Be Aware That You Have Blind Spots

I live in the country, and everything I do is about five to ten miles away. To get where I'm going, I have to make a left-hand turn out from my road. It's a treacherous turn because there's a hill that juts out right in front of the road, blinding you to oncoming traffic. You can't see the cars approaching from the left until the last minute. When my children were learning to drive, I drilled in their heads, a million times (or more), "Watch out for that intersection." Yet as long as I've lived in my home (close to 20 years), I have never seen an accident at this intersection. I think the reason is that it's so dangerous. People are extremely alert and cautious before they make that left-hand turn.

On the other hand, a little farther down that same road, there have been several fatal accidents because drivers failed to see a stop sign that was too small and easily missed. Blind spots, when you're not watching for them, can result in serious or fatal accidents. In the same way, our personal blind spots can be just as lethal.

For example, the apostle Peter was blinded by his pride (as most people are). He saw himself as more courageous than he actually was. Just before Christ's arrest, Jesus cautioned his disciples that they would all desert him. Peter believed he was the lone exception. He declared, "Even if everyone else deserts you, I never will." But Jesus knew Peter better than Peter knew himself. Jesus responded to Peter's bravado with these sober words, "I tell you the truth, Peter—this very night, before the rooster crows twice, you will deny three times that you even know me."

You would think that hearing Jesus' words would cause Peter to pause and recalculate. But he didn't. Peter didn't listen and confidently declared, No, Jesus, you're wrong, "Even if I have to die with you, I will never deny you!" And to give Peter a bit of a break, all the other disciples vowed the same thing (Mark 14:27-31 NLT). Yet less than 12 hours later, Peter denied Christ three times and all the other disciples deserted him as well. A very common blind spot is thinking that we're the lone exception to the rule. That we won't be the one to get a ticket for speeding or AIDS from unprotected sex or lung cancer from smoking.

Our biggest blind spots are our own pride and self-deception. The Bible tells us that "the human heart is the most deceitful of all things, and desperately wicked. Who really knows how bad it is?" (Jeremiah 17:9 NLT).

Our pride makes us unwilling to be taught, unwilling to be warned, and unwilling to be wrong, and because of our self-deception, we don't realize we're so unwilling and prideful. We just think we're seeing things as they really are. But the Bible says, "There is a way that seems right to a man, but its end is the way to death" (Proverbs 14:12 ESV). When we are closed to the influence of wise people in our lives, we're vulnerable to making poor choices.

Strong emotions cause significant blind spots. For example, when we feel furious with someone, we never see our own contribution to the problem. When we're "in love," we become blind to our lover's faults. Delilah deceived Sampson again and again because he was blind to her treachery (Judges 16:1-22). Unrestrained desire, lust, or incessant craving for something clouds our thinking mind. When we desire something strongly, we rationalize, excuse, and even lie to ourselves in order to have it. Individuals bound by addictions repeatedly tell themselves that it's not that bad, it's not hurting anyone, or that indulging in their particular addiction is actually helping them rather than enslaving them.

Listen to Others

When we start to take responsibility and admit we don't know everything or can't see everything, we are much more willing to invite others to speak into our lives. Proverbs says, "Get all the advice and instruction you can, so you will be wise the rest of your life…If you stop listening to instruction, my child, you will turn your back on knowledge" (Proverbs 19:20,27 NLT).

Often it is our family and close friends who see things we don't see and can warn us of danger ahead if only we will listen. Tim could have quickly rectified his situation had he listened to his mother. Instead he chose to pout and ended up making more bad choices.

Cheryl came to my office, afraid that she had made a terrible mistake. Newly married, her husband began verbally abusing her and her children. "I should have waited longer," Cheryl cried. "We only dated six months. But, I didn't know he was like this."

Cheryl was scared, confused, and angry with herself. She had already been in one abusive marriage, why would she repeat the same mistake? As we talked more about her dating history, it turns out she'd repeatedly made poor choices. In her words she said, "I put on rose colored glasses and refuse to take them off until it's too late. In my pride, I didn't listen to those who tried to warn me. Now, I'm in another mess and don't know what to do."

The painful consequences of her first marriage as well as abusive relationships in Cheryl's past didn't help her learn to recalculate the way she chose her dating partners or even who she found herself attracted to. Cheryl needs to learn why she is attracted to certain types of men and how she closes her eyes to the important clues that might reveal that charm on the outside is not the same as character on the inside. Kindness, empathy, honesty, gentleness, and patience are necessary for healthy relationships to flourish. From Cheryl's disappointment and heartache, she can learn the important lessons she needs. As she recalculates she will also gain greater self-respect and the skills she needs to invite her husband to make healthy changes as well (Proverbs 19:20).[4]

Learn from Your Mistakes

Like Cheryl and Tim, we all make mistakes, so stop beating yourself up when you make one. Instead, learn from them and work hard not to repeat them. When we find ourselves continuing in the same unhappy and unhealthy patterns we've always done, we must stop to ask ourselves, Why are we resisting the truth and what is our particular payoff for our continued foolishness?

It's tough to change old patterns, and most of us don't do so without the support of others. That is one of the purposes of the body of Christ. I wonder if Paul could have done all he did without the support and encouragement of Barnabas (Acts 9:27) or Timothy and Titus? We are to encourage one another (Hebrews 3:13) and build up one another. As I said in the introduction, I too am learning how to be a happier person. Sometimes change is hard, but it's so worth it when you succeed.

As I write this I am working on changing some unhealthy eating habits I've fallen into over the past several years. I've rationalized since I'm middle aged, the extra pounds and girth is inevitable. I find that much of my recreation and pleasure revolves around food. It's easier to eat cookies for lunch instead of soup or salad, but the consequences are making me feel unhappy. But instead of beating myself up, I'm learning to make wiser eating choices.

Accept Your Limitations

Making good choices isn't always easy. We're not always sure what the right decision is even when we know God's Word and try hard to follow it. Sometimes we don't know whether our particular decision will lead to happiness or heartache.

Samantha struggled with whether or not to reconcile with her husband. They had been separated for six months after she found out he'd been involved for several years with another woman. Her husband desperately wanted his family back. He was in personal counseling and met regularly with their pastor. He seemed like he was changing but how would Samantha know for sure?

Her mother sternly warned her not to take him back. "He's never been a good husband," she said. Looking back over her marriage, Samantha knew that in many ways her mom was right. Paul had been selfish, and she had enabled it, thinking that was her role as a good and submissive wife. His affair was the last straw. Was God truly at work? Should she give him a second chance? Reconciling their marriage would be best for their children. But what if he cheated on her again? She would feel so foolish.

Every human being makes mistakes. We're not perfect, nor are we ever going to be perfect. Samantha agonized over whether or not to reconcile with her husband partly because she told herself she wouldn't respect herself if it didn't work out. In other words, if she took him back and he reverted to his old ways, she would feel foolish and stupid for choosing to believe him and reconcile.

I told Samantha I could understand why she'd lose respect for her husband if that happened, but why would she lose respect for herself? From my point of view, she was making the best choice she could with the information available to her right now. She was looking out for the interests of her children and hopeful that God would restore their family. She wasn't making those choices blindly. They were both in counseling and had accountability partners who would help them stay the course of authentic healing and reconciliation of their marriage. Over a course of months, there was positive evidence that her husband was repentant, and he demonstrated the fruit of his changes in the way he treated Samantha and the children.

However, none of us knows for sure what will happen tomorrow, nor are there guarantees that things or other people will respond like we'd want them to. Samantha could do everything right and her husband could still act wrong. At times, we cause our own misery because we beat ourselves up if we realize that the choice we've made hasn't worked out the way we hoped it would. Again, the internal story line is that somehow we *should* be better than we are at being able to foresee the future and discern people's true motivations. But as finite human beings, we can't. That's God's job, not ours.

In a different situation, Larry came to a counseling session agitated and angry with himself. The day before, their washing machine broke down and his wife, Carole, suggested that since their washer was old, they go out and buy a new one. But Larry thought he might be able to fix it, and since they were short on cash, he went to the store, bought the part he thought it needed, and spent yesterday, his day off, installing the new part and removing the old one. The only glitch was the washing machine still didn't work.

Larry was furious with himself that he wasted his money and his time trying to fix the washer. "We still have to go out and buy a new one. I'm so stupid," he said. "I should have listened to Carole."

I disagreed with Larry's self-evaluation. I asked him, "If you had been successful at fixing the washer, how would you have felt?" He responded, "I'd have felt great and saved us a bundle of money."

"So Larry, you took a chance and tried to do something that didn't work. Why was that a bad choice? If it had worked, you would have been pleased. How can you know ahead of time the outcome of your efforts? Stop allowing things out of your control to rob you of your peace and joy."

Larry calmed down, accepted his limitations, and stopped berating himself. He did make the best decision he knew to make at the time, even if it didn't yield the results he'd hoped for. When we let go of our internal stories and unrealistic expectations about how things *should* go, we will experience life's disappointments in a more peaceful way. In other words, choppy waves on the surface of the ocean don't necessarily disturb the calm below.

Keep a Big-Picture Perspective

One of the most useful things we can do when making decisions is to recognize that our short-term perspective is limited and we might get a very different view when we add the wide angle lens to our decision making. Pleasure feels great but is gone the moment we stop satisfying our senses. The Bible warns us about the seductive pleasure of adultery. "For the lips of an immoral woman are as sweet as honey, and her mouth is smoother than oil. But in the end she is as bitter as poison, as dangerous as a double-edged sword" (Proverbs 5:3-4 NLT). It is often the temporal pleasures or satisfaction we seek that lead to the long-term pain and unhappiness we feel.

God has created humankind with the capacity to make decisions and a free will to make bad ones as well as good ones. Each of us has within ourselves a destructive force (sin nature) that attempts to keep us from the source of truth and light. As he did with Eve, Satan tries to beguile us by filling our belly with tasty versions of counterfeit joy, peace, love, and hope. He tries to get us to believe power makes peace, passion brings love, pleasure gives joy and popularity, prestige and possessions give hope and security. When we look at the moment, we easily forget the bigger story (or may not even know the real story). Thomas Merton says that "we cannot see things in perspective until we cease to hug them to our bosom."[5]

☙

When I got my new glasses recently everything came into better focus. Sometimes it's hard to see what is true truth. To be happy, we need a new way of seeing ourselves, life, and what's important. We need to learn to recalculate and surrender to God and learn his ways.

Back in the garden, Adam and Eve experienced a meaningful, joyful, peaceful, hopeful, and loving life. Because of their poor choices paradise has been lost. Sin robbed them and us of God's best. But God not only redeems us from the penalty of sin, he desires to restore us from the damage of sin. Let's learn how to see what God sees.

Questions for
Thought and Discussion

1. Could you relate better to Tim or Tim's mother? Have you been open to correction and recalculating your choices, or have you tended to blame others and wonder why your life is such a mess?

2. One of the first steps in making good choices is to take responsibility. Reread the poem "Autobiography in Five Short Chapters" on pages 84 and 85, and ask yourself which chapter you most often live in.

3. Reflect on this statement by Oswald Chambers. He writes, "We must learn to harness our impulses." He goes on to add, "We have the ability to fix the form of our choices for good or bad."[6]

How do you live this out in your daily life? Do you feel you are making good choices?

4. The chapter suggested several steps to making good decisions. Taking responsibility, being aware of blind spots, listening to others, learning from mistakes, accepting limitations, and keeping a big picture perspective. Which of these steps are strengths and which are weaknesses in your decision-making process?

5. Read Proverbs 20:17; 21:6; Jeremiah 13:17-22. What are some of the long-term emotional consequences of poor choices?

6. Read Proverbs 14:12-13. Discuss how our blind spots lead to unhappiness.

7. Many of us learn life's lessons the hard way. Read Proverbs 24:30-34. How might you learn by observing the life of other people? Pay attention to happy people. How do they make decisions and what kinds of decisions do they make? What about unhappy, grumpy people? What is their decision-making process, and what are the results?

8. Write down the steps of making good decisions. When your emotional brain lurches ahead, use your thinking brain to put the brakes on and slow your decision-making process down. If you have been in a habit of making poor choices, you will need to be intentional about learning how to make better (not perfect) choices. Start this week and pay attention to how much better you feel about yourself when you make a good choice or learn from a bad one.

PART TWO

• • • •

Moving Beyond
Our Unhappiness

CHAPTER 5

A New Way of Seeing

I believe in Christianity as I believe that the sun has risen: not only because I see it, but because by it I see everything else.

C.S. LEWIS

Happiness consists in finding out precisely what the one thing "necessary" may be in our lives and in gladly relinquishing all the rest.

THOMAS MERTON

There is nothing better than being wise, knowing how to interpret the meaning of life. Wisdom puts light in the eyes, and gives gentleness to words and manners.

SOLOMON, IN ECCLESIASTES 8:1 MSG

MANY YEARS BACK, I TOOK A CLASS from an image consultant, who helped me figure out what color clothing I should wear. She told me I was an *autumn*. That meant I looked my best wearing browns, oranges, camels, and beiges, and should accent these neutrals with rich jewel-toned fabrics like amber, emerald, and garnet. Gold jewelry was better than silver to enhance my skin tone, and I should avoid wearing anything black near my face. Clothes shopping became a breeze. I knew what colors worked and what didn't. For many years I thought I did look my best until I went to a professional speaking workshop where they had two image consultants evaluate our "look." Together they gave me the bad news. I was wearing all the wrong colors. I should not be wearing gold, but silver jewelry. And warm colors made me look faded and drawn. They said I needed more of the cool palette. Shocked, I refused to believe them at first.

Thankfully they persisted. They took pictures draping me in each fabric, warm and cool, and showed me how my skin tone looked more alive in the cool tones with silver jewelry. They even suggested I wear black, a color I always avoided. Ever so slowly my eye began to see what they meant. When I went home I started wearing a few things in the colors these consultants recommended. People complimented me on how I looked. I didn't hear "You look tired" as often. Eventually I was convinced. They were right. Over time, I changed my entire wardrobe.

Not too long ago, I was sorting through some old photographs and I now see clearly how those warm colors were not flattering on me. But how come I didn't see it before? It's interesting how our internal beliefs shape what we "see" and don't "see." When I believed that the warmer colors were the right ones for me to wear, I saw myself looking good in them. Later on, with the help of photographs and other people, I could now see that what I thought was true—wasn't. It's important to understand that our perception *is* our reality and only changes as we are open to new facts or ideas and believe them as truer than what we thought earlier.

⟡

Thus far, I have been challenging our typical way of seeing how life is supposed to work. We have all believed that more of something will give us the happiness and peacefulness that our heart longs for. I'm hoping that you are beginning to see that this idea isn't true and are becoming more and more open to what God says about experiencing the abundant life.

Jesus was all about changing the way people saw things. He wanted them to view God, themselves, and their Jewish faith from a fresh perspective. God knows our human blind spots as well as our proclivity to become deceived. Jesus told people,

> Your eye is a lamp that provides light for your body. When your eye is good, your whole body is filled with light. But when your eye is bad, your whole body is filled with darkness. And if the light you *think* you have is actually darkness, how deep that darkness is! (Matthew 6:22-23 NLT).

Jesus directly confronted the religious leaders' internal beliefs about who God was, how he worked, and what was important to him. For example, the Pharisees believed that rigorously keeping the Sabbath was one of the most important things a devout Jew should do. The Pharisees became outraged when Jesus violated Sabbath rules by healing people. Jesus wanted the religious leaders to know that caring about the well-being of a person didn't violate God's Sabbath, it actually demonstrated God's love. But the Pharisees would not believe it. They were blind to seeing things in a new way. (See Matthew 12 or Luke 14 for examples.)

Jesus constantly challenged the Jews' perceptions and beliefs. An expert in Jewish law asked Jesus what he needed to do to inherit eternal life. Jesus answered him with another question, "What is written in the law? How do you read (see) it?"

The man answered correctly, saying, "Love the Lord your God with all your heart and with all your soul and with all your strength and with all your mind and, love your neighbor as yourself." But wanting to justify himself, he asked Jesus, "Who is my neighbor?"

Jesus responded by telling a story about a man who was beaten, robbed, and left for dead. Jesus said a priest saw the injured man, but instead of stopping and offering to help, he crossed over to the other side of the road. The same thing happened again with a Levite. Finally a Samaritan man saw the wounded man, took pity on him, and helped him, thus fulfilling the Jewish law to love your neighbor as yourself (Luke 10:25-37).

The point of Jesus' story wasn't simply that loving one's neighbor meant we should stop and help an injured person. The question "Who is my neighbor?" was used to show the Jews something entirely new. In Christ's day, Samaritans were deeply despised by the Jews and seen as inferior, yet Jesus cast the Samaritan man as the hero of the story. Jesus said he was the *only* one who loved his neighbor. The Jewish priest and Levite did not. Jesus wanted to change the way people looked at things; he turned them upside down and inside out, and the religious leaders didn't like it one bit.

In another instance, this Jewish man, Jesus, took the time to have a private conversation with a woman. This was unheard of in Jewish culture. Not only was she a woman, she was a Samaritan woman, an immoral woman, and currently living in sin. Even his disciples were astonished at this break in cultural protocol. After they talked and Jesus offered her living water, he commissioned her, an immoral, Samaritan woman to be an evangelist to her own people (John 4:28-39). How outrageous! But the people of her town listened to her story and many believed.

Jesus ate meals with tax collectors, prostitutes, and sinners. Imagine your elders and church leaders' response if your pastor regularly (or even once) dined with drug lords, prostitutes, pedophiles, and pimps. The Pharisees believed that they saw God rightly through the law of Moses—but Jesus said they couldn't have been blinder (see Matthew 23).

• • • • • • The Upside-Down Perspective • • • • • •

Jesus told the following story to some "who had great confidence in their own righteousness and scorned everyone else":

Two men went to the Temple to pray. One was a Pharisee, and the other was a despised tax collector. The Pharisee stood by himself and prayed this prayer: "I thank you,

God, that I am not a sinner like everyone else. For I don't cheat, I don't sin, and I don't commit adultery. I'm certainly not like the tax collector! I fast twice a week, and I give you a tenth of my income."

But the tax collector stood at a distance and dared not even lift his eyes to heaven as he prayed. Instead he beat his chest in sorrow, saying, "O God, be merciful to me, for I am a sinner."

When he was finished, Jesus said, "I tell you, this sinner, not the Pharisee, returned home justified before God. For those who exalt themselves will be humbled, and those who humble themselves will be exalted" (Luke 18:9-14 NLT). The religious good guys weren't so good after all. And the ones labeled the bad guys received God's grace.

• •

Wisdom: Seeing Things as They Really Are

Thus far we have learned that much of our unhappiness results from wrong thinking and wrong habits, not always situational factors. Therefore, we must open ourselves up to the right ways of seeing, perceiving, and thinking so that we can develop habits that lead us to a greater sense of joy, peace, hope, and love. The Bible tells us that we begin this change process by renewing our mind (Romans 12:2). This does not mean replacing negative thoughts with biblical truths (although that is a start). Renewing our mind requires an entire overhaul. We need a new way of seeing ourselves, God, life, and what really matters. The psalmist David says, "With you is the fountain of life; in your light we see light" (Psalm 36:9).

In the light, things look very different than they do in the dark. For our honeymoon, my husband and I decided to go to Colorado to ski. We arrived late at night and drove up the mountain to our lodge. We skied Monday through Friday and left to drive back home early

Saturday morning. Winding our way down the mountain slope along the steep cliffs terrified me. Driving up the mountain at night felt harmless because I couldn't see the danger. Now, in the light of day I saw everything clearly. I enjoyed the breathtaking beauty of the view, but felt close to panic whenever my eyes fell on the precipitous edge we were driving along. In a similar way, living in God's light opens our eyes to the pitfalls and dangers and teaches us to recognize true beauty as well as what really matters. In the dark, we are much more vulnerable to being deceived and making foolish choices because in the dark, we aren't aware that the edge is so close.

Back in the fifteenth century, people used to believe that the sun revolved around the earth. When Copernicus discovered that wasn't the case, it changed everything. It revolutionized the way scientists viewed the entire universe. No longer was the earth the center.

Like the people in Copernicus's time, in our culture, we think we see things as they really are, but our human perspective is limited and it sometimes borders on craziness. We have viewed ourselves at the center of our own universe. We arrogantly live as if there is no God that we are accountable to or as if God revolves himself around us, blessing us, meeting our needs, and giving us a ticket to heaven to use later.

But as Copernicus discovered that the earth revolved around the sun, we too must come to see and accept that we are not the center of truth or life, or even the main character of our story. God is, and he doesn't revolve around us. We are here to glorify, love, and please him. When we live with that reality in the forefront of our minds, everything looks differently to us. From that perspective, we can learn what God says will bring joy, love, peace, hope, and happiness to our heart. We know he is the center of what is true, good, and right, and we want to follow him.

Jesus calls all people everywhere to repent and believe. Repentance isn't just turning away from sinful behavior, it's turning away from our futile and empty way of seeing things. It's turning away from ourselves as the center and turning toward God. When we see clearly, we see the world's value system and sin as it really is; it looks irrational and foolish, even if it feels good or sparkles.

While at a doctor's appointment recently I was browsing women's magazines. I came across a short blurb announcing a new, limited-edition handbag in a beautiful metallic finish, for a price tag of $2700. When asked the logic behind designing such an expensive bag when people are cutting their spending, the designer responded, "In challenging times, I think people want to surround themselves with things that are personally meaningful and enduring."[1]

He's right. We do want to surround ourselves with things that are meaningful and enduring, but how could we think that an expensive purse provides those things? How foolish and blind we have become that we actually fall for the hype of Madison Avenue advertisers over God's Word? Perhaps for you it's not a $2700 purse, but a $300 purse that you just have to have because it makes you feel important and that you're successful enough to afford such an item.

Don't get me wrong. I'm not opposed to buying some beautiful things to enjoy or wear. But don't think for a moment that they will give you anything meaningful or enduring. They are just things. God surely wants us to have a meaningful and enduring life but it's not found in expensive handbags or anything else that we could possibly buy. You would find more meaning and enduring pleasure if you donated your extra $2700 to feed starving children, provide housing for orphans, or help a missionary bring Bibles into a closed country.

When we see clearly, we understand that knowing God and loving him isn't boring or restrictive, it is beautiful and desirable and exceedingly good. It changes everything for what we need to find authentic happiness.

Putting on God's Glasses

Many of us have read the Bible as a textbook, trying to understand the lessons we need to learn. Or we've seen the Scriptures as a rule book telling us what we can and cannot do in order to gain God's blessing for our lives. A.W. Tozer writes,

> The Bible is not an end in itself, but a means to bring men to an intimate and satisfying knowledge of God, that they may enter into Him, that they may delight in His Presence, may taste and know the inner sweetness of the very God Himself in the core and center of their hearts.[2]

The Bible is not to be read as a rule book or textbook, but a storybook. It tells us God's account of creation, brokenness, redemption, resurrection, reconciliation, and restoration as well as of his future return. God wants us to understand the larger story behind our own personal narrative and it puts our lives into a context of a much larger drama.

After creating humankind from the dust of the earth, God placed Adam and Eve in paradise, a garden that grew lush foliage, delicious fruit, and dazzling flowers. Adam and Eve experienced God's presence and enjoyed his friendship. They were holy and happy. But God knew that as creatures, Adam and Eve were incapable of discerning good and evil apart from him. What looked good to the human eye (the juicy fruit from the forbidden tree) God knew was harmful. That's why he told them the truth—that they would die if they ate from the tree of the knowledge of good and evil (Genesis 2:17).

The story of human brokenness begins when the serpent questioned the validity of God's words. The serpent told Eve, "God's not telling you the truth. You will not die." The Bible tells us that the forbidden fruit in the Garden of Eden was a delight to the eyes and it was desired to make one wise. By eating it the serpent promised Eve that it would give her more wisdom and more knowledge than God had already given her. In fact, she would no longer be merely a creature, she would become as wise as God. (See Genesis 3 for the story.)

It looked good and sounded appealing, but it wasn't the truth. At that moment, however, instead of trusting God's words to help her evaluate what was good and right, Eve trusted in her own sense of things to know what would be best for her. She ate the fruit and invited Adam to eat it also. They indeed got more, but it didn't lead to their happiness. Adam and Eve now experienced uncomfortable self-consciousness, shame, fear, and marital discord. They lost their sense of oneness with themselves, with one another, and with God. They were promised something wonderful but it turned out tragic.

Satan's goal is the same today as it was in the garden. With clever deception he tries to convince us that God's words are not to be trusted and that if we believe God, we will be gypped out of something pleasurable and desirable. As he did with Eve, Satan causes us to question God's goodness by telling us that there is something better for us than what God has already provided. Adam and Eve's decision to doubt God's goodness, as well as to question his words led to disastrous consequences.

Recently I was talking with one of my clients about his health. When we were talking about the possibility of taking off some weight he said, "I don't want to have to deny myself anything. That feels bad and I feel gypped out of something good." At the moment, my client was blind to the reality that Satan was deceiving him with the lure of food just as he did with Eve.

At one time or another we have all bought into Satan's lie that more (food, love, expensive purses or cars, status, power, toys, sex, money—something other than God) will give us greater love, peace, pleasure, meaningfulness, and happiness. But it wasn't true for Adam and Eve, and it is not true today. Social scientist David G. Myers, in his book *The American Paradox,* writes,

> We now have, as average Americans, doubled real incomes and doubled what money buys. We have espresso coffee, the World Wide Web, sports utility vehicles, and caller ID. And we have less happiness, more depression, more fragile relationships, less communal commitment, less vocational security, more crime (even after the recent decline), and more demoralized children.[3]

Adam and Eve learned, albeit too late, that they were deceived. The serpent looked like the good guy, genuinely desiring Eve's best interest and he painted a picture of God as someone not to be trusted. If we want to find the only source for lasting joy, peace, love, and hope, we will need to start our journey by settling the questions "Is God good?" and "Is what he tells me true?" not only for our spiritual life but for our entire well-being.

Is God Good?

It's tempting to think that we only struggle with the question of God's goodness when things go wrong in our lives. But as we've just learned, Eve doubted God's goodness even in the midst of paradise. For both Adam and Eve life was good. There was no suffering to tempt Eve to doubt God's character, and yet still she decided not to submit to God's truth or trust his goodness when she ate the forbidden fruit. Honest people acknowledge that they often struggle to believe God's goodness toward them while they're suffering. But it's equally important to grasp that many times we don't trust and obey God simply because we think we know better and want to be in charge of our own lives.

The Scriptures repeatedly tell us that we are not to lean on our own understanding and that there is a way that seems right to us, but in the end it leads to death (Proverbs 3:5; 14:12). Because of this human blind spot, it is crucial that we think through the question of God's goodness because throughout much of our lives we will be tempted to believe that God is *not* good, or that we know better than God does what we need to find lasting happiness.

The answer to the question, "Is God good?" isn't easy for many people to answer, even as Christians. Sometimes my clients ask me how a good and loving God could allow thousands of innocent people to perish in the terroristic attacks on September 11, 2001, or to be swept away in the tsunami of 2004? Each week our national news reports incidents of rape, murder, children being trafficked into sex slavery, greed, and corruption. It's difficult to comprehend why a good God permits evil to flourish. The short answer is we don't know.

The Assault of Pain and Suffering

In the previous chapters, we've looked at pain and suffering through the lens of our own poor choices. But trials and heartaches come to all of us in one form or another and many times they are totally outside our own control. A father with four young children is diagnosed with a brain tumor and dies, leaving his wife and children struggling to make ends meet. A couple invests their entire life savings with a Christian businessman only to learn he has defrauded them of their retirement. A beautiful young woman was sexually abused by her father most of her childhood and her mother did nothing to stop it. Is God good when he permits agony and affliction and evil to thrash the lives of those he says he loves?

The biblical account of Job's life is difficult for us to wrap our minds around. In the first chapter, God gives us a glimpse into the larger story line behind Job's tragic losses and physical afflictions. Satan enters God's presence in order to accuse Job of hypocrisy. "Job's godliness is self serving; he is righteous only because it pays. If God will only let Satan tempt Job by breaking the link between righteousness and blessing, he will expose the righteous man for the sinner he is."[4]

God allowed Job to be tested to prove Satan wrong. We're glad that God had confidence in Job's integrity, but knowing that God permitted Satan to severely test Job's love and loyalty by orchestrating great suffering doesn't comfort us; it scares us. Is God good when he allows his loved ones to be used as pawns in a cosmic battle? How can we trust him?

During a particularly painful period in my life I severely questioned God's goodness. After becoming pregnant with our first child, my husband was diagnosed with a rare form of cancer. The treatments would hopefully provide a cure, but it would leave us unable to have any more children. At the time, I was simply grateful for being pregnant and having hope that my husband would be around to raise our child. But after a few years, my heart longed for another baby. Through a series of amazing circumstances, God supernaturally orchestrated an opportunity for us to privately adopt a newborn. The birth mother was quite sure she did not want this child and she agreed that we could adopt it. Arrangements were made and we eagerly awaited her phone call when she was starting labor. The phone call never came.

A week past her due date, I sensed something was terribly wrong. After another week I couldn't stand waiting and I called a mutual friend and asked the dreaded question, "What's going on?"

After a long pause, she said, "Leslie, I don't know how to tell you this. She gave her baby boy to a different couple to adopt."

"What?" I dropped to my knees and felt the air escape from my lungs, my heart sank, and my faith crumbled. I could have handled the baby's death easier than I handled the mother's deception. After all we had been through, how could God have allowed this to happen? Why did he bring us to this woman? Why did it seem like this was his perfect will only to snatch it from our hands? Why me? Why this? Why? Why? In that moment, I judged God and he was not good.[5]

When pain and suffering assault us, I know I'm not alone in my confusion. The Bible is full of questioners and questions. Jeremiah doubted God's goodness from the depth of the pit (Lamentations 3); Asaph struggled trusting God when he saw the good guys suffering and the bad guys flourishing (Psalm 73). Elijah told himself his entire ministry was a waste when God didn't change the hearts of King Ahab and his queen Jezebel after the dramatic encounter on Mount Carmel (1 Kings 19). After he was imprisoned, John the Baptist questioned whether Jesus was really the Christ, even after he declared him to be so when he baptized him (Luke 7:20).

God is not angry with our doubts or our questions. He invites us to freely come to him and ask. The problem we have is that we don't always like his answers or we simply can't understand his ways or his purposes in allowing evil and suffering in this world. We have a hard time trusting in God's goodness when the moment we're in feels so bad.

• • • • • • • • • • **What Is Good?** • • • • • • • • • • •

Goodness is a moral question, not a scientific one. Who gets to define what is good? When I judged God as not good when the private adoption failed, or I thought my father was not good for limiting my candy and dragging me to the dentist, I made my own view of things the highest authority. But what makes my judgment any truer than the next person's? What if what I define as good, someone else sees as bad? Is there any absolute authority that teaches us how to view things or is everything seen through the eyes of our own perspective?

In his *Systematic Theology,* Dr. Wayne Grudem wrote, "The good-ness of God means that God is the final standard of good, and all that God is and does is worthy of approval."[6] But it's not *our* approval that defines what good is, it is *God's* approval. The Scrip-tures define and declare that God is good and that what he does is good. (See Psalm 100:5; 106:1; 34:8; 119:68; 86:5; Nahum 1:7.) Jesus also affirmed God's goodness when he told the rich young ruler, "No one is good—except God alone" (Mark 10:18). A.W. Tozer writes,

> The goodness of God is that which disposes Him to be kind, cordial, benevolent, and full of good will toward men. He is tenderhearted and of quick sympathy, and His unfailing attitude toward all moral beings is open, frank, and friendly. By his nature He is inclined to bestow blessedness and He takes holy pleasure in the happi-ness of his people.[7]

• •

Before we can see things from God's perspective we will need to trust that God is good and he knows best. On the surface, things are not always what they seem to be. What often looks good to us, turns out to be bad, and what feels bad to us often turns out to be good. When I was a child I loved eating candy. It tasted much better than meat, rice, or even french fries and fruit. I ate so much candy my teeth decayed.

But going to the dentist felt painful, so I never wanted to go nor would I have chosen to. Thankfully I had a father who saw beyond my foolishness and made me eat healthier and get my teeth fixed. It was good to do so. Now that I'm grown and more mature, I can see that, but at the time I didn't understand. I just thought my father was being mean.

In the same way, many times we can look back over the worst of times and see that they were also some of the best times of God's goodness toward us. We see his provisions or experience his presence in deeper ways. From the vantage of history, we see that what we thought was bad, God used for good. In the Old Testament story of Joseph, we learned that he was able to keep his peace and hope alive in the midst of circumstantial hardship because he knew that God's purposes were always good (Genesis 50:20).

Major and Minor Themes

One of the things that helped me see God's goodness differently during the painful loss of the baby was when I read these words, "God is light, and there is no darkness in him at all" (1 John 1:5 NLT). The apostle John declared that this was the message he heard from Jesus and that he wrote these things down so that we might have joy (1 John 1:4). The psalmist said, "You are not a God who delights in wickedness, evil may not dwell with you" (Psalm 5:4 ESV).

In my anger and pain, I was not only blaming God for doing bad things, I was accusing God of being evil. He tricked me and deceived me. As I pondered John's words about God's character, I was forced to decide whose truth was true. If God is incapable of darkness, then God is incapable of evil. He is *all* good *all* the time. If that was true, then there had to be another reason God allowed my personal pain and suffering. There is a mystery to the Almighty that we cannot expect to grasp with our finite minds. Perhaps I would never know his purposes this side of eternity but would I trust that God knew, and that he was indeed good?

In the book *Faith and Culture Devotional*, John Eldredge refers to two main themes woven throughout Scripture, "A major theme of hope, love, and life triumphant, and a minor theme of suffering, sorrow, and loss."[8] He says when people focus only on the major theme of Scripture we can sound insensitive and glib about the real hardships of those who hurt, promising them that God will work all things for good and that they can have victory in Jesus. He says, "The Christianity that talks only about hope, joy, and overcoming would be hollow, syrupy, shallow."[9]

On the other hand, he cautions us that in modern culture's quest for authenticity and transparency, the church has majored in the minor theme of brokenness and suffering. Although refreshingly honest and necessary, if that is all there is, where is our hope? Where is the abundant life that Jesus promises? Where is the resurrection, the redemption, the restoration and reconciliation themes of Scripture? Eldredge concludes, "We must be honest about the minor theme, but we must keep it the minor theme."[10]

Do You Believe Me?

Jesus knows this world is full of trials and hardships. Throughout the four Gospels, Jesus repeatedly tells people that he is telling them the truth. Yet what they heard from Jesus was so different from what Jewish people were used to thinking and believing that for many, it wasn't easy to recognize as truth even when they wanted to. The father whose son was demon possessed begged Jesus, "I do believe, *but* help me overcome my unbelief" (Mark 9:24 NLT). Belief and unbelief isn't either/or, it's both/and. We believe *and* we doubt. But the more we believe the more we can trust. Richard Rohr says, "The opposite of faith isn't doubt, it's anxiety."[11]

Imagine you were playing a game where you already knew the outcome. You know that in the end, your team wins. Would knowing that fact ahead of time make a difference in your attitude when it seemed like the other team was ahead? Or when you dropped the ball or got knocked down? When you already know your team wins, it doesn't remove the pain or struggle. It doesn't mean you don't make critical errors or the taunts from the other side don't hurt. But knowing your team wins, sure helps remove the fear of losing and gives you a special hope and an inner joy that no matter what it looks like in the moment, you know your team wins!

Throughout his ministry, Jesus rarely answered any seeker's question directly. Most often he responded with a question of his own or a story. But in one particular passage he does answer directly. When asked "What must we do to do the works God requires?" Jesus answered, "The work of God is this: to believe in the one he has sent" (John 6:28-29).

Believing God takes work. The psalmist prayed, "Give me happiness, O Lord, for I give myself to you. O Lord, you are so good, so ready to forgive, so full of unfailing love for all who ask for your help" (Psalm 86:4-5 NLT).

Do you believe it? If so, it changes the way you see everything and you start to fall in love with God.

Questions for
• • • • • •
Thought and Discussion

1. Imagine attending a retreat with a number of other strangers. Once there, you are escorted to your room. It is plain and unadorned. There are no mirrors in the bedroom or bathroom. You are then instructed to remove all your rings, jewelry, and makeup (if you're a woman) and to place them in your suitcase. For the rest of the weekend you are to wear jeans, a plain white shirt, and flip-flops (which you were told to bring).

   When you gather with all the other retreat participants, you are told *not* to share your last name or what you do for a living. In other words, this weekend you simply have to be you, with no props or identification tags like PhD or CEO. You do not have external ornaments to set yourself apart like a Rolex watch or a designer purse or shoes that say, *Look at me, I'm special* or *I'm successful.* For the entire weekend, you have to be just plain unadorned you. The retreat leader gives you some specific things to talk about and to do together to get to know one another in real ways.

- How would you feel? Why?

- How dependent are you on external things (like what you do, wear, or own) to define you and make you feel special or important?

- After sharing an entire weekend together with no props or pressure, just real talk and fun and meaningful activities, how do you imagine you'd feel? Do you think you'd feel freer and happier? Why or why not?

- How might such an experience help you "see" things or people in a new light?

2. Read Luke 4:18-19. What did Jesus set us free from? What does he want us to see?

3. Read Habakkuk chapter 1. The prophet questioned God's goodness in the midst of moral treachery. Yet in the end, he chose to trust in God's goodness. Read chapter 3, verses 17-19. Faith is trusting God, even when you can't see what he's up to. Will you choose to believe?

4. Get a hymnbook or look up the words on the Internet to the hymn "Day by Day and with Each Passing Moment" by Lina Sandell Berg. Meditate on the hymnwriter's trust in God's goodness. Lina was the daughter of a Swedish pastor. When in her mid-twenties, she accompanied him on a ship journey to the city of Gothenburg, but before they arrived, the ship lurched, and he fell overboard and drowned before her eyes.[12] Have you ever had to trust in God's goodness even when the circumstantial evidence pointed otherwise?

5. Slowly read Psalm 86:5. Take some time to meditate on this verse, word by word. How have you struggled with God's goodness? Where do you not believe him? How does that cause anxiety, guilt, or other happiness robbers in your life?

6. Read Psalm 56, especially verse 9, and Romans 8:31-39. How would you feel different if you knew God was for you and that he loved you?

CHAPTER 6

Fall in Love

Now God designed the human…to run on Himself…
God cannot give us a happiness and peace apart from
Himself, because it is not there. There is no such thing.

C.S. LEWIS

You cannot taste and see how gracious the Lord
is, while you are hungering for gold.

BERNARD OF CLAIRVAUX

MY MOTHER WAS THE YOUNGEST OF SIX CHILDREN, a fiercely independent woman. Her mother, my grandmother, was hospitalized soon after my mom's birth due to postpartum depression. She remained institutionalized most of her life. My mother's early history is sketchy but I was told she was taken care of by her oldest sister (who wasn't happy about the task) and as soon as my mother turned 18 years old, she married my father. They had three children and after nine years of marriage, she divorced my father. I was eight years old, my sister four years old, and my brother was only two.

Mom took us to live in an apartment in Chicago. She struggled as a single parent. By the time I was 14 years old, she lost custody of us because of her drinking and abusive behavior and we went to live with our father, his wife, and her three children in the suburbs.

I tell you this because after we moved to my father's house my mother chose not to have much to do with any of her children. Occasionally she would take us for a visit but over time that stopped. She didn't attend our weddings, or see any of her grandchildren when they were born, or know when my husband and I adopted our daughter from Korea. We never spent any holidays with her. Eventually she remarried and moved to another state. For over 15 years, I never even spoke with her.

෯

All that changed for me one day when my sister Patt received a phone call from our mother asking for help. Patt had reestablished some contact with her, but Mom had never asked to see me. Now our mother was ill and was asking Patt what she should do. Patt advised her to go to the hospital and promptly called me, inviting me to go with her to see our mother.

Over the 15-year absence, I had worked to heal from the hurt and fallout of my mother's abusive behavior. I let go of my expectations that she would ever change and forgave her, but we had never reconciled. Mom was unwilling to see anything she had ever done that had hurt me. Now Patt was asking me to accompany her to see our mother. I was unsure of our mom's reaction to seeing me, but I assured my sister that I would go to support her.

When we got to the hospital, I was scared. Had I grown enough in my faith to handle being provoked and not reacting? Was my forgiveness genuine? It's easy to think you've forgiven someone when you don't have to see them again. But when I saw my mother, I felt God's amazing grace filling my heart with his love for her. She looked so small and fragile in her hospital bed.

We soon discovered that she was in a fight for her life. Being a smoker for many years had a price—it's called lung cancer. I had no expectations of a mother-daughter relationship, but I determined to minister to her with God's unfailing love. When she made a disparaging remark, I ignored it and instead offered to comb her hair or smooth lip balm over her parched lips. And the amazing thing was, she allowed it.

Mom understood that she was in a battle that was bigger than she could handle alone. Her pride might have moved her to refuse our care, but she did not. Instead she accepted it and even began to enjoy it. My mother clearly understood her neediness, and she did not allow her independence or even her shame to keep her from receiving our assistance.

Although my mother was acutely cognizant of her need for tangible aid, she wasn't as conscious of her need for love, mercy, and forgiveness. But my sister, brother, and I offered her those things alongside the physical help. I often thought to myself how much humility it took for her to allow us to love and care for her. To receive it she had to acknowledge her helplessness and dependence. She also knew very well she hadn't been a good mother. This extravagant love and care was not owed her. Yet she drank it in like a dry sponge soaks up water. She once said to us, "You're too good to me. I don't deserve this," and she was right. As she felt her need and allowed our love, mercy, and grace to nourish her, her bitter and parched spirit began to flourish. Love was changing her. Her body was dying, but the last year of her life was the most alive she had ever been.

The Good News of the Gospel Is Unbelievably Good

Many times we don't seek God's love or forgiveness because we do not recognize or admit our desperate need for it. We think we're doing just fine on our own even though the truth is that we're hopelessly lost and desperate. Other times, we may acknowledge our need but feel so undeserving and unworthy of God's love or his forgiveness, we can't receive it or feel it until we can figure out a way to make ourselves worthier. But the gospel of Jesus Christ gives us hope and good news. The truth is there is not a thing we can ever do to make ourselves worthy enough to receive God's grace nor could we ever earn it. Who could stand before God and honestly say, "I deserve your love and forgiveness"?

These extravagant gifts from God don't depend on our goodness or worthiness anymore than the love and care we extended to my mother depended on her being a good mother. They are gifts, not rewards for good behavior. As with any gift, however, it must be received in order to be experienced by the recipient and we can't receive it if we won't first face our neediness.

In the Scriptures, Jesus had a conversation with a young man who thought he had what it took to be worthy. Jesus showed him how impossible it was for even a good person to be good enough. Let's look at what he said.

> As Jesus started on his way, a man ran up to him and fell on his knees before him. "Good teacher," he asked, "what must I do to inherit eternal life?"
>
> "Why do you call me good?" Jesus answered. "No one is good—except God alone. You know the commandments: 'Do not murder, do not commit adultery, do not steal, do not give false testimony, do not defraud, honor your father and mother.'"
>
> "Teacher," he declared, "all these I have kept since I was a boy."
>
> *Jesus looked at him and loved him.* "One thing you lack," he said. "Go, sell everything you have and give to the poor, and you will have treasure in heaven. Then come, follow me."
>
> At this, the man's face fell. He went away sad, because he had great wealth.
>
> Jesus looked around and said to his disciples, "How hard it is for the rich to enter the kingdom of God!"

The disciples were amazed at his words. But Jesus said again, "Children, how hard it is to enter the kingdom of God! It is easier for a camel to go through the eye of a needle than for a rich man to enter the kingdom of God."

The disciples were even more amazed, and said to each other, "Who then can be saved?"

Jesus looked at them and said, "With man this is impossible, but not with God; all things are possible with God" (Mark 10:17-27).

The story of the rich young ruler is about God's extravagant love and our insufficiency and inability to ever be good enough to gain eternal life or to enter the kingdom of God. When the young ruler approached Jesus, it was about what he could do. He already thought he kept the Mosaic law. He asked Jesus, "Aren't I good enough?" Jesus gently raised the bar again and again but each time the young ruler confidently asserted that he already did that.

Finally, Jesus said, "Here's one thing you lack," and told him to give away all of his money. Jesus wanted this young man to recognize his neediness. His wealth kept him blind to his brokenness. Jesus knew that this new task was beyond this young man's personal ability to carry out. Rather than humbly confess his helplessness and beg for Jesus' help, he walked away sad.

The disciples were speechless. Jesus then turned to them and asked, "How hard is it for the rich to enter the kingdom of God?" They didn't know how to respond. Jesus asked them again because he wanted to make a point that they would never forget. *It's impossible!* In this story, Jesus taught his disciples that people with money are easily deceived into thinking that they are self-sufficient. For a wealthy person, the world's system works, and it's almost impossible for a rich person to recognize his or her interior poverty. Jesus likened it to the task of threading a camel through the eye of a needle.

Hopeless, the disciples ask Jesus, "Then who can be saved?" Jesus' answer surprises his disciples with the incredible good news. He tells them that humanly it is impossible, but with God, all things are possible. Jesus declares God does it, not us. Even a good person cannot be good enough. To receive what God offers us, however, we have to own our helplessness and be willing to receive.

Too Good?

For many people this is most challenging. We don't like receiving an extravagant gift if we have nothing to give in return. We feel extremely uncomfortable accepting a kindness from someone when we can't reciprocate. I buy spare Christmas presents every year just in case someone surprises me with an unexpected gift. I don't want to feel empty-handed.

· · · · · · · · · · · **Accept the Gift** · · · · · · · · · · ·

Last summer I went to get a pedicure. I informed the nail technician that I didn't want a leg massage—which is standard—because I had active poison ivy on my legs. Despite my request, she lathered up her bare hands with a rich emollient and started to gently massage my infected legs (and she did understand English). Horrified, I started to protest and pull away until I looked into her eyes and heard the Holy Spirit's still, small voice telling me to receive this gift of kindness. How could I? She was a total stranger who was willing to put her bare hands on my infected legs. I was so moved by her compassion, I had to hold myself back from weeping.

· ·

Our pride and shame can be so powerful. Our neighbor offers to bring over a meal when we're sick, but we graciously decline. We'd rather eat a can of cold soup than be seen as needy. We don't want to receive something if we don't feel we deserve it, or have earned it, or can return the favor. For many of us it's easier to give than receive. It makes us feel better about ourselves.

Jesus showed the rich young ruler what his problem was and what he needed to *do,* but he would not lower himself enough to receive what only God could give him. Jesus tells us, "Blessed are the poor in spirit, for theirs is the kingdom of heaven" (Matthew 5:3). We cannot be filled up with God when we are still full of ourselves. The rich young ruler was in bondage to his self-sufficiency and wealth and wasn't willing to be set free. François Fenelon said, "Golden chains are no less chains than chains of iron."[1]

Wealthy individuals aren't the only ones deceived and in bondage to chains of gold. Those who do not personally possess wealth still believe that it is the answer to their problems and if only they had more, all would be well. They too are blind to the reality that materialism, money, pleasure, and power can never give them lasting happiness. Jesus tried to help this rich young man see that he needed God more than he needed his money but he was unwilling to put God in his rightful place in his heart. His problem wasn't that he didn't love God at all, but that he loved his money more.

We're not unlike that rich young man. It may not be money that has bound us, but all of us have sought our well-being and happiness in god substitutes. God directed the prophet Jeremiah to write of Israel, "My people have committed two sins: They have forsaken me, the spring of living water, and have dug their own cisterns, broken cisterns that cannot hold water" (Jeremiah 2:13). Yet Jesus says, "If anyone is thirsty, let him come to me and drink" (John 7:37).

Disordered Loves

The biblical account of the rich young ruler richly illustrates two important truths. The first one we've just covered. God's love for us is solely and completely because of his grace and not because we've done something right. The second truth is about what we love and what we love the most. The rich young ruler thought he was keeping the Jewish law, but he was blinded to the reality that he failed to follow the most important one, "You shall love the LORD your God with all your heart and with all your soul and with all your might" (Deuteronomy 6:5 ESV). What he loved most was exposed when Jesus asked the rich young ruler to give up his money and follow him.

Please hear me. Jesus was not teaching that money is evil or that everyone needs to give it all away in order to be a follower. If that were the point of the story, then it would be something we could do to earn God's merit. Having a lot of money can be good and used for great and noble purposes. It is the inordinate love of money, or anything else that takes the place that only God should occupy, that corrupts our heart. What we love the most controls us and changes us (2 Corinthians 5:14; Hosea 9:10b).

Let's look at this concept of disordered loves in the context of human relationships. Recently my daughter, Amanda, got married. When she fell in love, she began to change. She was more thoughtful, less selfish. She stopped flirting with other men. She wasn't interested in anyone else; her heart was committed and devoted. Her fiancé's needs and wants became important to her, and she made her future decisions in life through the lens of her love for him. It's not that she didn't love her parents, her brother, her dog, or girlfriends, pizza, or chocolate anymore, but she didn't love them the most. They were lesser loves, as they should be. But her marriage would be in trouble if she put these lesser loves in her husband's place. Even more disastrous to the well-being of her marriage relationship would be putting another man in the place of her heart that only her husband should occupy.

In the same way a spouse wants to be the first love in his or her beloved's heart, God wants to have first place in our heart. Throughout the Scriptures, God lamented that Israel chased after other loves instead of resting in and enjoying his love. He calls it spiritual adultery, and it breaks his heart (Jeremiah 9:2; Ezekiel 6:9).

Having a good marriage takes a lot of work. No one drifts into intimacy. It takes time to get to know one another, build deep trust, and share one's dreams and feelings. Any good relationship must be nurtured and maintained or it will drift apart. Yet, often in our busy lives we neglect our human relationships in pursuit of our other loves. Or we ask of them more than is possible. Our loves are out of order. Oswald Chambers writes,

> If we love a human being and do not love God, we demand of him every perfection and every rectitude, and when we do not get it, we become cruel and vindictive; we are demanding of a human being that which he or she cannot give. There is only one Being who can satisfy the last aching abyss of the human heart and that is the Lord Jesus Christ. Why our Lord is apparently so severe regarding every human relationship is because he knows that every relationship not based on loyalty to Himself will end in disaster.[2]

I've often wondered why God commanded us to love him first and foremost. It's not because he is lonely or needs our love. Unlike us, God is totally self-sufficient and needs nothing from his creatures to be more than he already is. He commands us to love him with everything that is in us because he knows that loving him is in our absolute best interest. It is good for us to love him most because he knows that we are lost and we won't find true happiness without him.

As Christians, our problem usually isn't that we love the wrong things, although some people do love things that are harmful and destructive like drugs, illicit sexual relationships, or pornography. The objects of our affections are usually good, not sinful in and of themselves. To name a few, we love ourselves, our spouse, and our children, we love our homes, we love having a good time, we love beauty and nature, we love our friends and family, we love to eat, we love our pets, we love good chocolate, we love to be loved, we love to be respected, and we love having some control over our world.

God doesn't want us to stop loving other things. We were created to love and be loved, and God made things in this world for us to desire and enjoy. He called them good. He sternly warns us, however, not to make secondary things primary and primary things second-ary. Our problem usually isn't what we love but that our loves are out of order. Lesser loves have stolen our heart. It's not only that we love other things too much, but we love God too little. To the church in Ephesus, the angel wrote, "You have persevered and endured hardships for my name, and have not grown weary. Yet, I hold this against you: You have forsaken your first love" (Revelation 2:3-4).

Like the church at Ephesus, we can do many good and right things and still forget God. God doesn't ask us to love *only* him, but he com-mands us to love him first and most and tells us to order all our other affections and desires around our love for him. In his excellent book *Reordered Love, Reordered Lives: Learning the Deep Meaning of Happi-ness,* David Naugle writes,

> The happy life, then consists of learning how to love both God supremely and the world in the right way at the very same time. In fact, the world and its resources exist to point us to God and his glory, that we might recognize God in, and love him for, his gifts.[3]

Disordered Lives

The consequence of having our loves out of order is a disordered life. We love things and use people. We say we love God, but our hearts long after something else that we think will fill us up or make us happy. Naugle writes,

> We can all too easily confuse what we desire with what is desirable, satisfy the superficial and starve the essential traits of our nature, love absolutely what we should love relatively, and love relatively what we should love absolutely. We can be on a fool's errand after fool's gold.[4]

By ourselves we can't accurately discern what is in our best interests.

Isn't that what happened to Adam and Eve in the garden? First Eve, then Adam thought they knew better than God what they needed. As it was then, today deception is still a part of the process and as a result of our disordered loves, our very natures have become damaged (Romans 7:18). The Bible tells us that we confuse evil things with good things and wrong with right (Isaiah 5:20-21). The apostle Paul writes, "They exchanged the truth of God for a lie, and worshiped and served created things rather than the Creator" (Romans 1:25).

Paul is warning us that because of our damaged natures, our human leaning is to worship people and things more than we worship God. As in Christ's day, we have all been blinded by the values of a worldly kingdom and fervently seek them, rather than God, for our happiness, peace, and well-being. Like many of the religious people in Christ's day we say we believe in God and know Jesus died for our sins, but what we think will make us happy is God plus something from the world's kingdom. Henri Nouwen, noted author and theologian, journaled his own struggle in this regard. He wrote,

> I want to love God, but also make a career. I want to be
> a good Christian, but also have my successes as a teacher,
> preacher or speaker. I want to be a saint, but also enjoy the
> sensations of the sinner. I want to be close to Christ, but
> also popular and liked by people. No wonder that living
> becomes a tiring enterprise.[5]

No wonder indeed!

The Struggle Between Two Kingdoms

When I was a child, one of our favorite neighborhood games was called King of the Mountain. The strongest and usually the oldest kid would get to the top of a large dirt pile and everyone else's goal was to knock him (or her) down and take their place as the new king. When we got to the top, it would be our turn to feel big and powerful and in control, until the next kid overpowered us. It felt great when I got to be on the top of the mountain, but even at the top, I had no peace because I knew that sooner or later, I would get pushed down again.

In his book *In Pursuit of Happiness: Finding Genuine Fulfillment in Life,* James Houston writes, "We first need to recognize that probably our most basic choice in life is between power and love. Either we choose power or we choose love as our first priority in living."[6] If we want greater happiness in life, it's time to reevaluate what's ruling our life. Is it power and the quest for control over people and things, or is it love?

Below are descriptions of two opposing kingdoms. Jesus has rescued us out of the domain of darkness and brought us into the light (Ephesians 5:1-14). Look at the characteristics of each kingdom below. Imagine yourself living your life more fully in the kingdom of God. How would you feel? It's clear to see which kingdom brings greater joy, peace, hope, and happiness. If you are in Christ, you are set free from the kingdom of darkness, but do you live in that reality of freedom or are you still in bondage?

Kingdom of God	Kingdom of Darkness
freedom	bondage
love	fear
generosity	selfishness
humility	pride
surrender/submission	power/control over others
contentment	craving
gratitude	complaining and grumbling
grace	condemnation/criticism
peace	conflict/war
forgiveness	revenge/bitterness
justice	oppression/power
mercy	hatred, apathy, indifference

When we live primarily in the kingdom that values power over love, anxiety or anger will always be our default mode, never peace and happiness. Never forget this important truth. Even if we feel strong and powerful ruling our own kingdom by having money or being popular or influential, deep down inside, we know those things don't last forever or bring inner joy. The writer of Ecclesiastes had all these things and more. He was the king and on top of his mountain, and in spite of this he reminds us that these things are ultimately empty. Sooner or later the power is gone and there will be someone better than us to take our place.

• • • • • • • • • • **What Will Last?** • • • • • • • • • •

Karen came to see me for counseling because of chronic anxiety and general unhappiness in her life. She was married with two athletic, popular children, but she constantly worried that jealousy from other kids and their parents would rob her kids of their opportunities for playing time and team membership. In addition, she thought that the women in her neighborhood didn't like her and that she felt hurt that she was not invited to their social events.

Karen attended a wonderful church and had plenty of opportunities to serve the poor, go on missions trips, be generous with her time as a stay-at-home mom as well as lovingly care for her family. But instead of living joyfully, loving God, and loving others, she was ruled by fear because she felt powerless to achieve the level of acceptance she craved that would assure her children's continued athletic achievements. Even when she got invited to a neighborhood party and her children played first string on the team, she couldn't feel happy because she was anxious that it wouldn't last.

And she's right. Nothing lasts forever in the world's kingdom. That's why Jesus tells us to store up for ourselves treasures in his kingdom (Matthew 6:19).

• •

Jesus challenged the world's value system at every turn and made it crystal clear that we can't serve both kingdoms at the same time

(Matthew 6:24). We will either bow down to the kingdom of power and money and everything those values represent, or we will love God first, and out of his fullness dare to love others in a way that draws them toward Christ.

Heather had a promising career ahead of her after graduating from college. Instead of seeking a great job making lots of money so she could buy nice stuff, she decided to abandon the kingdom of the world and live courageously by faith in God's kingdom of love and light. Currently she works in a ministry that seeks to rescue women out of the pit of the pornography industry. Heather walks into hell with the torch of Jesus brightly shining. Instead of a comfortable life, she's found a meaningful and abundant one.

Jesus told his followers to seek his kingdom and his righteousness *first,* not only because it is right for us to do so as God's creatures, but also because it is good for us. God has hardwired our bodies as well as our spirits to feel joy-filled and wonderfully alive when we live in tune with our Creator and his values and purposes. When we refuse, we not only stay spiritually weak, we cause harm to ourselves. God lamented to the psalmist, "How long will you love delusions and seek false gods?" (Psalm 4:2).

Jesus told his followers, "The thief comes only to steal and kill and destroy; I have come that they may have life, and have it to the full" (John 10:10). It is loving God first and most; living in his kingdom of light that makes everything else easier to discern.

Setting Love in Order

How do we love God the most? First, we need to see ourselves truthfully. We are not as sufficient as we think. We have all gone our own way and loved other things more than we've loved God (Romans 3:11-12). We need to wake up to how desperate we are for his mercy, love, and forgiveness.

Second, we need to see God more clearly. As we come to know this holy God, we see that he is beautiful, desirable, lovable, and worthy of all our heart, our mind, our soul, and our strength. We discover to our complete amazement and joy that he wants to generously give us his love, his grace, his mercy, and his forgiveness, even though we don't deserve it. And so, our heart can't help but respond back with love. When someone does something for you that is costly and sacrificial, it does endear you to him or her.

Third, loving God is demonstrated by surrendering our will to him and obeying him. Jesus said that if you love him, you will keep his commandments (John 14:15). When we believe God's words are good for us and essential to our well-being, we don't *have* to listen to and obey God, we *want* to.

Several years ago my spiritual director gave me something to ponder. I have read it often. It says,

> Nothing is more practical than finding God, than falling in love in quite an absolute, final way. What you are in love with, what seizes your imagination, will affect everything.
>
> It will decide what will get you out of bed in the morning, what you will do with your evening, how you spend your weekends, what you read, whom you know, what breaks your heart, and what amazes you with joy and gratitude. Fall in love, stay in love, and it will decide everything.[7]

ᕱ

Have you fallen in love with God? Like the rich young ruler, Zacchaeus, a tax collector, was a man who loved money more than anything else. We know this because tax collectors earned their living by extorting fellow Jews. The more they extorted, the richer they became. Zacchaeus was the chief tax collector and a wealthy man.

When Jesus passed through Jericho, Zacchaeus climbed up a tree in order to get a glimpse of him because Zacchaeus was short in stature and thick crowds lined the streets. Unlike the rich young ruler, Zacchaeus was *not* a good man but Jesus noticed him, asked him to climb down, and invited himself over to Zacchaeus' house.

Those who heard Jesus' words were astonished. "Jesus is going to the home of a sinner!" they exclaimed. But something happened in Zacchaeus' heart in that short encounter with Jesus. He woke up and saw himself clearly. He was a needy man. He felt the mercy and love of Christ overwhelm him and in that moment, his loves shifted. Zacchaeus didn't love his money the most anymore. We know this because he says in front of everyone, "Look, Lord! Here and now I give half of my possessions to the poor, and if I have cheated anybody out of anything, I will pay back four times the amount" (see Luke 19:1-9).

The sum must have been substantial, but Zacchaeus didn't care. His heart had fallen in love with someone far more wonderful than his gold, and it had changed everything. Zacchaeus was finally happy.

Questions for
• • • • • •
Thought and Discussion

1. Is it difficult for you to receive a kindness from someone else? Why or why not?

2. If you have been stuck needing to feel worthy in order to feel God's love or receive his forgiveness, what would make you feel worthy? What makes you more *unworthy* than anyone else is?

3. Do you agree or disagree with the author's statement that loving God first and most is in our best interests?

4. Reflect upon this statement by George Macdonald in his book *Discovering the Character of God*. He writes,

> Many doubtless mistake the joy of life for life itself. Longing after the joy, they eventually languish with a thirst at once poor and inextinguishable. But even that thirst points to the one spring. Those who mistake the joy of life for life, love self, not life. And self is but the shadow of life. When it is taken for life, and set as the man's center, it becomes a live death in the man, a devil he worships as his god.[8]

5. How do you use God as a means to happiness instead of having God be your happiness?

6. John Piper writes, "Preferring anything above Christ is the very essence of sin. It must be fought."[9] What love normally takes first place in your heart? How can you fight it in order to give God his rightful place?

7. What do you think Jesus meant when he said, "Seek first his king-dom and his righteousness, and all these things will be given to you as well" (Matthew 6:33)?

8. Paul is concerned for the Galatians when he says, "What has hap-pened to all your joy?" (Galatians 4:15). Experiencing the fruit of the Spirit are the blessings of living in sync with God's kingdom and his purposes. Mike Mason writes in *Champagne for the Soul,* "I know I've lost sight of the gospel when I find myself restless, unhappy, fearful, plagued by subtle guilt. Unhappiness keeps me stuck. Only joy moves me over the line into experiencing the king-dom of heaven."[10] How do your emotions warn you that you're living in the wrong kingdom for the wrong values and wrong purposes?

9. Have you fallen in love with God? If not, what still holds first place in your life?

CHAPTER 7

A Beautiful You

> We must diligently search into and set in order both
> the outward and the inner man, because both of them
> are of importance to our progress in godliness.
>
> THOMAS À KEMPIS

> I choose goodness…I will go without a dollar before I take
> a dishonest one. I will be overlooked before I will boast. I
> will confess before I will accuse. I choose goodness.
>
> MAX LUCADO

> Empower me to be a bold participant, rather than a timid
> saint in waiting; to exercise authority of honesty, rather
> than to defer to power or deceive to get it; to influence
> someone for justice, rather than impress anyone for gain;
> and by grace, to find treasures of joy, of friendship, of
> peace hidden in the fields you give me daily to plow.
>
> TED LODER

HUMAN BEINGS INSTINCTIVELY LOVE BEAUTY. The ability to create and appreciate beauty is crucial to our happiness because beauty draws our heart toward God. Who hasn't stood in awe and wonder at the foot of the Grand Canyon, or marveled at the mystery of the monarch butterfly?

Most of these magnificent creatures live only four to five weeks, but in autumn, their lifespan expands exponentially. They are nature's Methuselah (a Bible character that lived to be over 900 years old), and during this season live seven or eight months. In addition, these creatures know instinctively that in the fall they must start their journey to central Mexico. Miraculously, they are hardwired by God with an internal GPS (global positioning system) and fly over 50 miles a day to a place they've never been before in order to hibernate over the cold months. Come late February, they mate and in spring, fly all the way back to the United States and Canada.[1] Amazing.

It is God alone who embodies absolute beauty and everything he creates is beautiful. He delicately embroiders a bird's feathers with a mosaic design. He dapples the landscape with butterflies and flowers and decorates the night sky with sparkling diamonds. In his book *The Evidential Power of Beauty,* Thomas Dubay writes,

> The acute experience of great beauty readily evokes a nameless yearning for something more than earth can offer. Elegant splendor reawakens our spirit's aching need for the infinite, a hunger for more than matter can provide.[2]

When we fall in love with God, we have been captured by his beauty and glory, grateful for his loving grace, and we want to be like him. Yes, sin has damaged God's creation but has not completely destroyed its beauty. There are now thorns and thistles in the garden (and in our inner lives), but God longs not only to redeem us from the ugliness of sin, but to restore humankind to its intended beauty. What does a beautiful person look like?

Most women I know want to be as beautiful as possible but focus most of their efforts on their physical appearance. At the bare minimum, before they leave their house they wash their face, brush their teeth, and comb their hair. For those of us who require more energy to be attractive, we shower, put on our "face" and lipstick, and wear clothes that help us to feel more positive (thinner, that is). In addition, some of us may exercise, wax off our eyebrows and mustaches, color our hair, polish our nails, use wrinkle creams, and employ other unmentionables so that we feel as beautiful as we can.

We may not all agree on the ingredients that make a person lovely or handsome on the outside, but instinctively we all know what makes someone beautiful on the inside and that's what matters to God. Spiritual and secular people alike intuitively understand that beautiful individuals embody goodness, humility, honesty, kindness, courage, gentleness, patience, and self-control. They live in love and are not selfish or self-absorbed with their fame or their flaws, their good fortune or their failures. We cheer during movies such as *Gladiator* or *Braveheart* where goodness, courage, and love fights against cruelty, greed, and injustice.

Beauty or the Beast

Possessing talents, intelligence, and/or specific abilities are great blessings, but they are not indicative of inner beauty. They are window dressings, not character qualities. Our culture and even many churches publically praise those attributes but do little to teach people how to develop virtues. More often than not we are blind to the devastating and destructive effect of indulging our vices.

The Bible warns us,

> People will be lovers of themselves, lovers of money, boastful, proud, abusive, disobedient to their parents, ungrateful, unholy, without love, unforgiving, slanderous, without self-control, brutal, not lovers of the good, treacherous, rash, conceited, lovers of pleasure rather than lovers of God (2 Timothy 3:2-4).

These qualities do not describe an attractive person. What he or she loves is disordered and diseased and the end result of these choices is someone with no love at all. This person prefers evil over good and his or her soul is ruined. Dallas Willard writes,

The drive to self-gratification opens up into a life without boundaries, where nothing is forbidden—if one can "get away" with it. "Why?" is replaced with "Why not?" And because this is what these "gods" want—total license—God abandons them to a worthless or nonfunctional (*adokimon*) mind—that is, a mind that simply doesn't work.[3]

These individuals fail to see how their personhood has been degraded and the Bible describes them as blind, lost, wicked, and/or foolish. The apostle Paul warns,

Many walk, of whom I have told you often, and now tell you even weeping, that they are the enemies of the cross of Christ: whose end is destruction, whose god is their belly, and whose glory is in their shame—who set their mind on earthly things (Philippians 3:18-19 NKJV).

This passage describes people who are ruled by their emotional cravings and worldly appetites rather than by the love of God. You may not want to see yourself right now but you must. It's time to look in the mirror of God's Word and see how you're doing on your inner beauty. You might even ask your family or your closest friends. It is that important to your well-being and happiness.

I know it can be extremely painful to see who we are, not who we want to be, or pretend to be, or who others think we are, but who we *really* are. Sometimes I think I look fine but when I check myself in the mirror, I see that my lipstick is on my teeth or I have something disgusting hanging from my nose. When I didn't know it was there, it didn't bother me. But I'm glad I saw it. I'm even sort of thankful when someone tells me (although that is more humiliating than seeing it myself). We cannot correct something if we will not see it.

I've described the extremes of beautiful and ugly. Most of us fall somewhere in the middle. We are all in the process of becoming. The question you must face is, Which direction are you heading? Are you becoming beauty or the beast?

Becoming the Best Possible You

The ultimate makeover isn't done at the cosmetic counter, the gym, in a fancy department store, or by a plastic surgeon, but by God (Galatians 4:19). He works best, however, with our consent and our cooperation. We have to want it and be willing to be schooled in his classroom of inner-beauty development. There is no instant makeover, but if we want to be beautiful on the inside, it is well worth the cost. How much you want it is the question.

Desire

People have many desires and our desires are what give us energy, direction, and motivation for our life. For example, with one year of college under her belt, I asked Jane some of her inner longings. She said she wanted to continue college, but she also hoped to get her own apartment and live on her own for a while. Jane liked to party and keep late hours, but she said she also desired to love God (sort of). She yearned to be more physically attractive, she craved more attention from men, and she wanted to get good grades in her classes.

It's clear to see that Jane's desires often competed with and even contradicted one another. In pursuing one thing we long for, sometimes we must forsake another. Jane wanted to be more attractive and popular so she worked out at the gym and spent most of her money on makeup and clothes. The consequence of those choices was her finances fell short and she didn't have enough money to pay for her college textbooks.

I desire to be at a reasonable weight, but if I want that, then I can't eat everything I crave. If someone desires to be a good mom, she can't scream all the time or hit her kids whenever they aggravate her (although understandably she might feel like it in that moment).

This brings us to an important distinction between our deeper desires and our temporary feelings. Remember, we feel a lot of different things but the virtue of self-control helps us to not act out everything we feel, not only because it's wrong, but because it goes against who we are or who we want to work toward becoming. If our desire, for example, is to develop the virtue of patience, or courage, or honesty, when we feel irritated, or timid, or tempted to fib, we acknowledge our feelings or temptation, but we don't give in to them because if we do, we won't grow in patience, courage, or honesty.

The Bible has a lot to say about our desires. They can be good, bad, godly, or sinful. A perfectly legitimate desire can become disordered when it grows into a god for us or we try to make it give us something it wasn't intended to give us. We often do this in the realm of our relationships, especially marriage. When we demand or expect that another person meet all of our needs (and wants), or fulfill us and make us happy, we have put them in God's place, and we will always be disappointed.

Falling in love with God creates a new set of desires, ones that are not natural to the human heart. First and foremost, we now desire God to be God and not just our helper to come to our aid and give us what we want. In addition, we desire to know him and be like him. It makes us happy to make him happy and we want to glorify him by the way we live our lives. A.W. Tozer writes, "True spirituality manifests itself in certain dominant desires. These ever present, deep settled wants [are] sufficiently powerful to motivate and control the life."[4]

Below are some things that will help you grow your desire for inner beauty.

Pray for greater desire. For a long time in my own Christian life I thought that "being saved" meant my sins were forgiven and I got a ticket for heaven when I die. I continued to live my life for myself, with my ticket in my back pocket. I was grateful to escape hell, but was unaware that God designed much more. He wanted me to know him and to *want* to know him. Paul said that there wasn't anything more important to him than knowing God (Philippians 3:10). Jesus himself said that eternal life is knowing God (John 17:3). That doesn't start when we get to heaven—it begins right now. God desires our whole heart, and he longs for his people to *want* to love him with everything in us. He longs for us to *want* to serve him and to do good so that others will know him too.

• • • • • • • • • **Improving Our Tastes** • • • • • • • •

We understand intellectually that God's design is all good and that we should want him most, but truth be told, our heart longs after so many other things. We pursue him in the same way that we know we should eat more vegetables when what we really want is more dessert. We're still not seeing clearly. God is the best dessert. He is the whole meal. The psalmist declared, "Taste and see that the LORD is good" (Psalm 34:8).

Our desires are disordered and our taste buds damaged. It's like preferring to dine on a cheap cut of round steak when you have the opportunity to eat filet mignon. You don't desire filet because you've never tasted how good it really is.

• •

If your desire for God is weak, and longing for worldly things stronger, pray and ask God to increase your desire, your yearning and longing for him.

Keep company with like-minded persons. People influence us and affect our resolve. When I hang around women who gossip, I'm tempted to join in. When I am in the presence of truly beautiful, godly people, it creates in me a desire to be more like that. God tells us, "He who walks with the wise grows wise, but a companion of fools suffers harm" (Proverbs 13:20).

A baby will not grow into a healthy person without loving caregivers. In the same way, a Christian cannot grow to be beautiful without other believers who we can learn from, be encouraged by, accountable to, and imitate. Paul often tells people to imitate him and do what he does. (See, for example, Ephesians 5:1; Philippians 4:9.) That is how we learn best. Find some people who are beautiful and spend time in their company. They will help you desire God's beauty more, and you will be able to learn from their lives.

Be teachable. We don't know everything about everything we need to know. Don't let your pride keep you from receiving wisdom. You may need a new pair of glasses to see things clearly. Don't forget, we have an enemy who seeks to destroy everything beautiful, including us. He disguises himself as an angel of light and at first glance, may even appear attractive (2 Corinthians 11:14). We are easily deceived. That's why we can't always trust our own selves and we need God's Word and God's people to help us discern good from evil, wrong from right. There is a way that seems right to us, but the end is destruction (Proverbs 14:12).

For desire to move toward fruition, we must choose which of our many desires is most important and pursue it. Like Jane did, we often have opposing desires and it is helpful when we become more conscious of our inner war. The apostle Paul writes about our dilemma. He says,

> Live by the Spirit, and you will not gratify the desires of the sinful nature. For the sinful nature desires what is contrary to the Spirit, and the Spirit what is contrary to the sinful nature. They are in conflict with each other, so that you do not do what you want...
>
> The acts of the sinful nature are obvious: sexual immorality, impurity and debauchery; idolatry and witchcraft; hatred, discord, jealousy, fits of rage, selfish ambition, dissensions, factions and envy; drunkenness, orgies and the like...
>
> But the fruit of the Spirit is love, joy, peace, patience, kindness, goodness, faithfulness, gentleness and self-control.

Against such things there is no law. Those who belong to Christ Jesus have crucified the sinful nature with its passions and desires (Galatians 5:16-25).

Decision

Paul says that if we really want one thing, we will need to let go of another and that requires choosing who our inner master will be. Is it our flesh or is it the Spirit of God? Read again the passage above and notice the results of living to satisfy your fleshly desires as well as living ruled by the Holy Spirit. Which path do you think results in more beauty and greater happiness?

Each year thousands of people make New Year's resolutions. They usually desire to lose weight (after gaining weight over the holidays), and come January 1, make a decision to take it off. But most people do not follow through with their resolve. Remember, the body does what the body is most used to doing. Deciding to do something different isn't enough to actually do it different in the long run. Below are some things you can do to help your decisions become greater realities.

Tell someone. Be accountable. I was talking with one of my clients this past week who had decided to lose some weight. He was describing his food choices over the past few days and I asked him if he had told his wife of his decision? Sheepishly he said, "No, I didn't want her to know I was trying to cut back. I didn't want to hear her bust on me when I took a second helping of dinner or snacked on Doritos instead of Cheerios."

We laughed, but if he wants to lose weight, telling his wife would help. She could not only hold him accountable to his own goal, but she could help him avoid temptation by not buying certain items at the grocery store or preparing smaller and/or more nutritious dinners.

Make a plan. I've already told you I am a pessimist by nature. I'm also impatient. One area of great frustration for me is waiting. I especially hate waiting in long lines with slow clerks when I'm in a hurry. It's something that I hate in myself, and my impatience has made me look pretty ugly at times. These days I exhibit better self-control, meaning people don't see my ugly spirit as much, but I want to increase my ability to tolerate frustrating situations by having a peaceful countenance on the inside. That's my desire. I've shared this goal with my husband and some close friends. But I need a plan to actually work on it.

This is my strategy. When I stand in a long line and notice my body starting to feel irritated, I start to think positive and compassionate thoughts about the clerk. I pray for those in line with me, and take deep, slow breaths. I am happy to report that my plan is working. I am growing in feeling more peaceful inside even when my outer world is frustrating.

The best plan is one with specific, measurable steps. For example, if I want to have greater compassion and less anger toward my husband, I could make a list of all of his good points, and I could pray daily for his character development. I could make a list of all my ugly qualities that he has to live with so that I am more humble and less judgmental. When I feel impatient or angry with him, I could pray that God give me a compassionate heart and I could choose to forgive him promptly instead of brooding. Part of making a plan is knowing where your particular vulnerabilities lie and where temptation is strongest.

C.S. Lewis writes,

> Every time you make a choice you are turning the central part of you, the part of you that chooses, into something a little different from what it was before. And taking your life as a whole, with all your innumerable choices, all your life long you are slowly turning this central thing either into a heavenly creature or into a hellish creature.[5]

Decisions that have a plan and some accountability are best, but we also need determination to keep at it, especially when we fail.

Determination

James tells us that we all mess up and aren't perfect (James 3:2). What keeps us moving forward toward our goal is our determination to get there, one step at a time, persevering through obstacles and failure. We see the finish line and we want to get there, even if, for a season, it's two steps forward and one step backward.

Obstacles often appear as trials that God allows in order to strengthen our perseverance (James 1:3-4). We don't build significant muscle lifting tiny one pound weights. Lifting weights only builds muscle if we do it regularly and push ourselves to use the heaviest weight we can without injuring ourselves. In the same way, how do we develop patience if we're never put in frustrating situations? How can we build more self-control if we are never tempted? How do we trust God more if we never battle doubt?

The more serious problem I see people struggle with that keeps them from reaching their goal is how they handle failure. When they do not succeed in maintaining their resolve such as controlling their tongue, letting go of their negative emotions, breaking free from worry, or developing greater patience, instead of picking themselves back up and starting again, they give up. They tell themselves, *I can't, Nothing works, It's just not meant to be,* or *God's Word isn't true.*

Remember that *stinkin' thinkin'* we learned about in chapter 3? Before you learned to think in such negative ways, you didn't allow a little failure to thwart your goals. When you were about one year old, you desired to walk. You made a plan by standing up and holding on for dear life. Soon you tried letting go of the table and before you knew what happened, you plopped down on your bottom. Failure. But you didn't think of it in that way. You didn't tell yourself, *Give up, You're just a loser, You can't do anything right, Mom will just have to carry me throughout my life.* No, you were determined and got up and tried again. And, you fell down again, and again, and again, and again, until your body figured out how to balance itself without holding on.

Next came taking your first step. You started this task by holding on, perhaps to Mom's hand, and then falling down a couple of hundred times, and finally, your determination paid off. You did it. Everyone learns to walk. No one reaches the age of three without succeeding, unless there are neurological or physical limitations. As toddlers, we intuitively know that falling down is part of learning to walk. In the same way, as adults, we need to realize that failure teaches us many lessons we need in order to succeed. God wants you to become a beautiful person. That is his plan for you. You must not allow failure to stop you. Just get up again and learn what he has for you. Listen to what Peter, the apostle who failed, tells us. He writes,

> His divine power has given us everything we need for life and godliness through our knowledge of him who called us by his own glory and goodness. Through these he has given us his very great and precious promises, so that through them *you may participate in the divine nature* [beauty] and escape the corruption in the world [ugliness] caused by evil desires.
>
> For this very reason, *make every effort* to add to your faith goodness; and to goodness, knowledge; and to knowledge, self-control; and to self-control, perseverance; and to perseverance, godliness; and to godliness, brotherly kindness; and to brotherly kindness, love. For if you possess these qualities in *increasing measure* [it's a process], they will keep you from being ineffective and unproductive in your knowledge of our Lord Jesus Christ [give you a happy life] (2 Peter 1:3-8).

Last, but certainly not least, we need to know that we will have to practice what we're learning over and over again in order to build certain muscles into our lives that will empower us to fall down less, and stand up straighter so we will be more beautiful in our interior lives.

Discipline

We must never underestimate the power of a bad habit or the difficulty of building a new one. By nature we take the path of least resistance and if we do not train our mind, our emotions, our will, and our body, no matter how much we desire, decide, and are determined to do something, we still may not get there.

For example, let's say I want to run a marathon. Desire is a start, but it won't get me far unless I desire it more than other things, because running a marathon takes a considerable amount of time and commitment. Once I decide, I need a plan. I can't just sign up and go out and run for 26 miles. I don't even think I could walk that far in one day. How am I going to get my body, my mind, and my will to be ready to run a marathon? Even if I'm determined to run one, without consistent training, my legs and my physical heart won't be able to do what I desire. My body will collapse in an exhausted heap because I have not trained it to run in a way to finish the race.

The same process is true for developing character muscles that lead to inner beauty. The apostle Paul says that "everyone who competes in the games goes into strict training. They do it to get a crown that will not last; but we do it to get a crown that will last forever" (1 Corinthians 9:25). To be beautiful we must not only desire it, we must train ourselves to distinguish good from evil and prefer holiness to worldliness (Hebrews 5:14).

A popular television program on TLC is *What Not to Wear*. The program selects someone to receive a wardrobe makeover. At the time she is chosen, she has no idea that the way she dresses is extremely unflattering. Image consultants Stacy and Clinton work hard to help her see herself differently. Typically she resists. Her new clothes don't feel as comfortable and familiar as her old ones. But before too long, with a little encouragement, some good-natured teasing, and a lot of help, she is transformed from frumpy to fabulous.

God wants to give you a new wardrobe. Here's what it looks like:

Since God chose you to be the holy people he loves, you must clothe yourselves with tenderhearted mercy, kindness, humility, gentleness, and patience. Make allowance for each other's faults, and forgive anyone who offends you...Above all, clothe yourself with love, which binds us all together in perfect harmony (Colossians 3:12-14 NLT).

In Training

A few months ago I was attending my Sunday morning church service and behind me sat a young mother with four unruly children. Throughout the entire service they ran up and down their row, talking, giggling, squiggling, and squirming. It was impossible to ignore them. The children had not been trained to sit quietly during a church service. Their bodies were doing what children's bodies do. Squirm and be noisy.

I became aware of my growing internal irritation toward this mother who seemed oblivious that her children were disturbing the worship experience of everyone in her vicinity. In the past, my ugly self would have taken action to stop this disturbance, or else I would have brooded throughout the entire service about how inconsiderate this mother was and how unfair it was to the rest of us to have to endure this noise. I would have wanted some control over those children, over their ruckus, over their mother, and over my worship experience. I would have wanted to change the situation; instead God was changing me. He was making me more beautiful and training me how to feel peaceful on the inside while circumstances were stressful on the outside. The very thing I had been practicing while waiting in long lines.

Awareness of our inner ugliness is the first step of this new process of becoming beautiful. Action is the next step. I had to choose which way I was going to sit through the rest of the service. Was I going to revert to previous behavior to control this mother and her children in order to get my needs met or was I going to focus my energy on remaining peaceful inside and loving her and her noisy children, even if it was only in my thought life and with a warm smile and friendly handshake when we turned to greet one another?

Because I had been training, I found it easier in this moment to choose the path of love. I took a few deep slow breaths as God filled me with peacefulness and joy even in the midst of a noisy worship service. I felt happy during the rest of church even though I sensed the irritation of others around me growing. I knew their angst well. But I also knew I was breaking free from an old habit and it felt wonderful.

Remember, from chapter 2, my harrowing ride on the Cambodian elephant? The elephant did what his tummy wanted to do and in the moment his owner was helpless to control him. His pain at getting whacked in the neck did not stop him. Like the elephant's owner, I used to feel powerless over my impatience. It, not the love of Christ, controlled me, even though I knew it was ugly and I often felt guilty and unhappy with myself.

Professor and researcher Jonathan Haidt also uses a similar metaphor of an elephant and his rider in his book, *The Happiness Hypothesis*. Haidt explains the rider (or as in my example, the owner) as our rational, conscious mind, as well as our willpower, and the elephant as everything else (our emotions, our cravings and appetites, our habits, our past experiences and biological impulses). He says that the rider (our mind and will) isn't successful over the elephant if the elephant (everything else) isn't trained. When the elephant wants to go against his rider, the elephant wins every time because he is bigger and stronger. Haidt concludes, "The rider can be successful *only to the extent that it trains the elephant.*"[6]

The apostle Paul was not a psychologist, but he was on to something when he said, "I discipline my body like an athlete, training it do what it should. Otherwise, I fear that after preaching to others I myself might be disqualified" (1 Corinthians 9:27 NLT).

Positive thinking and willpower alone is never strong enough to be transformed into a beautiful person. For a complete makeover, Paul says, we must train ourselves to be godly so that inner beauty becomes more natural to us than ugliness (1 Timothy 4:7).

Training our mind, our emotions, our will, and our body to develop good habits is so crucial to becoming beautiful; in the next chapter I want to give you specific ways to do it.

Questions for
Thought and Discussion

1. How do you feel when you are in the presence of a beautiful person? How do you feel when you are with an ugly person?

2. John Piper writes, "God's work in us does not eliminate our work; it enables it."[7] Do you sense God's enabling you to become more beautiful? How?

3. Imagine you were told by someone you knew cared about you that you had bad breath or some offensive body odor. What would your response be? Of course you'd be embarrassed, but then what? Would you collapse into self-hatred or self-pity? Would you say, "Well, that's just the way I am—get used to it"? Or would you try to solve the problem?

Read Psalm 139:24, Proverbs 27:17, 1 Thessalonians 5:14, Hebrews 3:13, and Jeremiah 17:9.

Can you begin to do the same thing with your inner life when someone gives you feedback? Instead of hating yourself or defending yourself, can you start to take appropriate corrective action?

4. Read Psalm 52:3-4. In what way do our disordered loves make us ugly?

5. What character qualities of inner beauty would you like most to see develop in your life? What steps can you take to nurture and mature these?

6. Pay attention to how you feel after you've exhibited a virtue or indulged in a vice. To experiment, next time you feel impatient, counter it with an extra dose of compassion and kindness and see how you feel afterward. In addition, recall a time when you acted impatiently or rudely toward someone. How did you feel afterward? (Be careful. Sometimes we get deceived because we tell ourselves we're entitled to treat someone disrespectfully because they treated us wrong or they deserved it.)

7. Read Psalm 32:10-11 and Psalm 34. What is the difference between the emotional state of the wicked and the emotional well-being of the righteous?

8. Much of Christian theology focuses on *who I am in Christ*. But ask yourself, *Who is Christ in me?* Read Galatians 4:19. What would you look like if you allowed Christ to fully form himself in you?

CHAPTER 8

Training Elephants
and Human Hearts

*True peace of heart therefore is found by
resisting our passions, not by obeying them.*

THOMAS À KEMPIS

*If there is no struggle, there is no progress. Those who
profess to favor freedom, and depreciate agitation, are
men who want crops without plowing up the ground;
they want rain without thunder and lightning.*

FREDERICK DOUGLASS

*Give me understanding and I will obey your instructions;
I will put them into practice with all my heart.
Make me walk along the path of your commands,
for that is where my happiness is found.*

ASAPH, IN PSALM 119:34 NLT

JOSH AND SANDY FIDGETED IN THEIR SEATS while they told me what they hoped
to gain out of marital counseling. They had been together for five years
but were on the verge of separating. They felt hopeless and unhappy,
and said I was their last resort.

"I can't stand living like this anymore," Sandy cried. "We can't get along, our finances are a mess, and Josh is so moody, I'm getting depressed too."

"You make it sound like everything is my fault," Josh said defending himself. "It's just that whenever we try to change something, like Sandy's spending for example, it just doesn't work. We argue constantly, and sometimes it gets really ugly. I can't help that I get down when she criticizes me or the creditors are calling. Everything feels overwhelming."

"Tell me some things you've tried to do differently," I asked. "For instance, how have you tried to get yourselves out of debt?"

Sandy answered first. "We've stopped going to restaurants as much, and we're not putting more charges on our credit card, but it is hard to live that way. I hate to cook; we are used to eating out. I love to shop and feel depressed when I can't buy pretty things to wear or to decorate our house. I know I spend too much money, but there has to be a way we can get out of debt without totally depriving ourselves either."

Josh chimed in next. He said, "Anything we've tried never lasts very long. Sandy cooks dinner or doesn't spend money and I work to be in a better mood so we can get along, but it only lasts a week or two and then we're right back where we started. Nothing is working."

I asked them, "Was it working when you were working at it?" Both of them agreed it was. But they said they found it hard to maintain their momentum. Sometimes the pain of change makes us forget our former misery, and we revert to previous habits to feel better.

⟡

Feeling miserable with our self or our life can be positive when it motivates us to do something different. Often the motivation to change *only* comes when we are in desperate straits. Like Josh and Sandy did, we might try to make some changes in our spending habits or the way we handle things, but when the pain of change becomes great, we forget our former misery and often revert back to previous habits to feel better. Next, we might change jobs, change houses, or even change spouses in order to relieve our pain. Don't misunderstand me. There are times when changing our circumstances is the absolute best solution. Reducing situational stress provides some relief, but often it's only temporary.

Josh and Sandy were considering divorce, believing that seemed like the only thing that would solve their mutual misery. But if Sandy doesn't stop using money to feel better, she will still have problems with spending, debt, and creditors even if she is no longer married to Josh.

Josh hasn't learned how to control his emotions when he's upset, and reacts to stress with moodiness and anger. Even if Sandy is no longer his wife, life will never be perfect for Josh. When things don't go the way he thinks they should or wants them to, he will still get frustrated and depressed. If Sandy and Josh decide to divorce, they won't be happier in the long run because Sandy and Josh themselves will still be making the same choices that have brought them to this place.

In earlier chapters we've identified some areas that cause emotional turmoil and unhappiness. We've seen that God wants to restore our nature to be more like his and instructs us to put off bad habits and put on new ones (Ephesians 4:22-24). To do that takes training because change doesn't happen overnight and inner transformation doesn't occur quickly. Like Josh and Sandy, it might be unrealistic expectations, negative feelings, bad habits, or poor choices that we need to correct. We've also begun to see that many times we don't fully believe or trust God and instead we live hoping that the things of this world will give us the love, joy, or peace that our heart deeply longs for.

To move from where we are right now to where we want to be, we need some idea of where we want to end up as well as a vehicle to get there. That vehicle is self-discipline. Most of us don't like the word *discipline* because it conjures up memories of harsh punishments, humiliations, and deprivations from parents, teachers, coaches, and/or other authority figures from our past. But contrary to our initial reactions, please understand that self-discipline is crucial if you want to have a life well-lived. The opposite of disciplining ourselves isn't freedom, it is bondage. When we're undisciplined and out of control, we are slaves to our passions, our appetites, our ruling desires, and our emotions. We make a mess out of our lives and our relationships rather quickly and the consequences are not only unhappiness, but also self-hatred. Proverbs warns, "He who ignores discipline despises himself" (Proverbs 15:32).

There are three different kinds of self-discipline that help us become a happier person. There is the discipline of correction, the discipline of restraint, and the discipline of training ourselves to do the right thing at the right time for the right reason. Let's look at each of these more closely so that we can learn to build these critical disciplines into our daily life.

The Discipline of Correction

In chapter 2, we read about young Tim's misbehavior and his mother's attempt to get him to make different choices. It's important to note that it was not Tim's naughtiness that caused him the most difficulty. His initial misbehavior could have easily been corrected had he listened to his mother. Tim's mom warned him again and again, but he refused to stop his whining and complaining. Instead he continued to blame-shift and make excuses. Tim's unwillingness to receive his mother's correction led to more unhappiness when she implemented painful consequences for his disobedience. If Tim doesn't learn from these experiences how to value what godly people say to him and receive correction, when he becomes an adult, he will continue to be perplexed and angry as to why his life doesn't work and is such a mess.

As a counselor, I know it's impossible to work with people who refuse correction. They want the benefits of a peaceful and joyful heart but they don't want to do the things that God says take us there. They want loving, healthy relationships, but when they receive feedback on the hurtful things they do or say, they refuse to listen or to change.

● ● ● ● ● **The Wisdom of Heeding Correction** ● ● ● ● ●

Proverbs is a book about wisdom and learning to recalculate so that you can live a happier life. Here are just a few things it says about why the discipline of correction is crucial to our well-being.

> Blessed is the man who finds wisdom, the man who gains understanding, for she is more profitable than silver and yields better returns than gold. She is more precious than rubies; nothing you desire can compare with her. Long life is in her right hand; in her left hand are riches and honor. Her ways are pleasant ways, and all her paths are peace. She is a tree of life to those who embrace her; those who lay hold of her will be blessed (Proverbs 3:13-18).

> My son, pay attention to what I say; listen closely to my words. Do not let them out of your sight, keep them within your heart; for they are life to those who find them and health to a man's whole body. Above all else, guard your heart, for it is the wellspring of life (Proverbs 4:20-23).

> At the end of your life you will groan, when your flesh and body are spent. You will say, "How I hated discipline! How my heart spurned correction! I would not obey my teachers or listen to my instructors. I have come to the brink of utter ruin in the midst of the whole assembly" (Proverbs 5:11-14).

> These commands are a lamp, this teaching is a light, and the corrections of discipline are the way to life (Proverbs 6:23).

● ●

No one can make you change but you. People can tell you, they can warn you, they can plead with you, pray for you, and punish you. But if you refuse to listen, you will stay stuck doing the same thing you've always done.

Getting Unstuck

John came to counseling because, he said, "My wife will leave me if I don't change." For years she had been pleading with him to get help for his temper and verbal abuse. He would not listen. He knew better. Desperate, she told him she could not stand it anymore and informed him she was separating and taking the children to live with her parents. This crisis motivated John to make an appointment. Initially, John was not open to the discipline of correction. During our session he was argumentative and defensive. He blamed his wife for being unloving and not submissive.

Over time, however, John began to soften and eventually admitted that he wouldn't like being married to someone like him either. His confession didn't change John's temper or his habit of verbally vomiting all over his wife and kids, but it did make him much more open now to training himself to learn how to handle his ugly feelings without hurting those he said he loved.

You can choose to receive the wisdom of God and others or you can choose not to. You can decide to obey God or not. The discipline of correction is meant to help you not to humiliate you. But you must let go of your pride in order to receive it. The psalmist said, "Let the righteous strike me; it shall be a kindness. And let him reprove me; it shall be as excellent oil; let my head not refuse it" (Psalm 141:5 NKJV).

In addition to receiving correction from God and wise others, the discipline of self-correction means that we can (and do) recalculate when we see we've gone off course or fallen into the pit. Like we learned in chapter 3, emotional or relational pain is a huge red flag indicating that we are off course and need to make some changes. When we ignore the red flags, our problems don't go away, they usually get worse.

Angie felt like she was on the verge of a nervous breakdown. She was a single mother with three adult children who lived with her, but they continued to function as children. Angie worked full-time as a secretary and came home to cook and clean up after her adult brood. In return, they treated her with indifference and contempt. In order for Angie to start feeling happier with her life, she will need to make some crucial corrections in the way she allows herself to be treated.

The Pain of Change

Weekly I receive e-mails from frantic spouses and parents of adult children anxious to know how they can get their loved one to make better choices. Sadly I have to tell them that it's not possible to change another person. We certainly can influence people, but the only one we can actually change is ourselves. Throughout the Scriptures, God gives us his wisdom so that we will know what is best and choose his ways. But sometimes we blatantly refuse God's correction then wonder why our lives still don't work (Psalm 50:17).

For others, who—like Josh and Sandy—want to learn God's ways but are so deeply entrenched in bad habits, change can be very slow even when we're open to correction and want to change. When the Israelites were slaves in Egypt, they were eager to be set free from their bondage. God longed to give them a new life in the Promised Land, and they were anxious to have it. But once they left Egypt and travailed in the desert for a season, the pain of change became more real than their painful memories of toiling for the Egyptian taskmasters. Before long, the Israelites began to grumble and complain against God, telling Moses that they wanted to go back to Egypt (Numbers 11:4-5; Psalm 106:13-25). They hungered for the cucumbers and leeks, the garlic and onions of their old life. They remembered the pleasures of Egypt and forgot the pain of slavery.

In a similar way, our misery is often the push that moves us forward to seek God's pathway and accept the discipline of correction. As Josh and Sandy soon discovered, as we begin to make changes, the pain of struggling to do something new becomes greater than the memory of our bondage. Even though Sandy hated that she was in serious debt, sick that creditors were hounding her, and brokenhearted that Josh and she fought constantly, she found it nearly impossible to budget her money and curb her impulse spending.

Josh also tried to be more upbeat and control his angry outbursts, but the pain of change felt harder to both of them than the misery of their situation. Thomas à Kempis wrote,

> There is one thing that draws many back from spiritual progress and fervent improvement; dread of the difficulty, or rather the labor of the combat. However, they improve most in virtues, who strive like men to overcome these things which are most grievous and contrary to them.[1]

For Josh and Sandy, the consequences of their financial mess, their unhappy marriage, and emotional and marital distress were warning them that significant changes were needed. They knew that. In order to maintain their resolve to do it differently and actually succeed in making lasting changes, they also needed to train themselves in the discipline of restraint.

The Discipline of Restraint

The discipline of restraint teaches us to say *no* to ourselves in the moment of temptation. We have learned, often painfully so, that when we give into our temporary emotion, desire, or fleshly appetite, it often causes another problem, distracts us from our goal, leads to heartache, or ruins something else that we want.

Sara hasn't learned to control her tongue. She says whatever she thinks at the moment, with no thought as to how her barbed words will wound people around her. She humiliates her husband, John, and children and justifies it because in her mind they were foolish or wrong. She's in counseling now because she's losing her relationships with people she loves. No one wants to be near her. Why would they? It's like trying to wrap your arms around a cactus; it always hurts to be close.

Sara has begun to receive the discipline of correction by acknowledging how her reckless words cost her. People flee when she's in a bad mood. No one shares honestly with her because of her reactions, and she's unhappy, not only with them, but with herself. She feels ugly.

Many of us can relate with John and Sara, Josh and Sandy. We've justified our temper tantrums, excused our excesses, pampered our pity parties, and rationalized holding on to bitterness and resentments, all to our own peril. I hope you are seeing by now that hanging on to your immature and sinful ways of thinking, feeling, and behaving takes a serious toll on your relationships and happiness. Credit card debt, obesity, sexual promiscuity, pornography, broken relationships, drug abuse, and alcoholism are some of the results of our failure to discipline ourselves. Proverbs warns us, "The evil deeds of a wicked man ensnare him; the cords of his sin hold him fast. *He will die for lack of discipline,* led astray by his own great folly" (Proverbs 5:22-23).

We have wrongly bought into the lie, *If it feels good, do it. If I want something, I should have it.* And *If I deprive myself of some important felt need, I will be unhappy.* Back in the 1950s Rabbi Abraham Joshua Heschel recognized this cultural slide into self-centeredness and self-absorption when he wrote,

> Needs are looked upon today as if they were holy, as if they contained the quintessence of eternity. Needs are our gods, and we toil and spare no effort to gratify them. Suppression of desire is considered a sacrilege that must inevitably avenge itself in the form of some mental disorder...We feel jailed in the confinement of personal needs. The more we indulge in satisfactions, the deeper is our feeling of oppressiveness. We must be able to say *no* to ourselves in the name of a higher yes.[2]

What is the higher *yes* that we need to keep in mind so that we are empowered to say *no* to ourselves? Beauty! Freedom *from* slavery to our cravings, feelings, wants, and yes, even needs as well as the freedom *to become* who we were created to be. We can have incredible peace and joy available to us when we are no longer tossed about by our unruly flesh, our negative emotions, other people, or even difficult circumstances. Something or rather, someone greater than ourselves anchors us even in the midst of temptation, fear, and personal turmoil (see Colossians 3:1-18).

The apostle Paul instructs us on the importance of the discipline of restraint for right now as well as for later. Scripture reminds us that the rewards of heaven are real and worth waiting for. For that reason alone we should say *no* to things that will rob us of our beauty and our eternal rewards. Paul wrote,

> The grace of God that brings salvation has appeared to all men. It teaches us to say "No" to ungodliness and worldly passions, and to live self-controlled, upright and godly lives *in this present age,* while we wait for the blessed hope—the glorious appearing of our great God and Savior, Jesus Christ, who gave himself for us to redeem us from all wickedness and to purify for himself a people that are his very own, eager to do what is good (Titus 2:11-14).

The discipline of restraint is not only necessary in order to say *no* to sinful or harmful things, but it also trains us to say *no* to good things that can rob us of God's best. We'll look more closely in the next chapter how busyness with even good things can keep us preoccupied and stressed and instead of trusting God, we're performing, striving, and exhausted.

Learning Restraint

The quickest way to train yourself in the discipline of restraint is to practice the spiritual discipline of fasting. We often think of fasting in relation to prayer and fasting for some specific need. But the discipline of fasting means you purposefully deny yourself food, or some other thing you want for a time or season. The regular practice of fasting helps us learn that our cravings (wants, needs, desires) don't *have* to have dominion over us. For example, when you skip lunch or an entire day of food, your body cries out *Feed me, I'm hungry*. Saying *no* to your flesh teaches and eventually trains your body to obey your will and the Holy Spirit. Dallas Willard says,

> Persons well used to fasting as a systematic practice will have a clear and constant sense of their resources in God. And that will help them endure deprivations of *all* kinds, even to the point of coping with them easily and cheerfully... Fasting teaches temperance or self-control and therefore teaches moderation and restraint with regard to *all* our fundamental drives.[3]

One of the first steps many individuals take when learning to break free from sexual addictions is a period of sexual abstinence (fast). Sexual addicts need to learn that their sexual cravings, although powerful, don't have to be acted on each time they feel them. The same process is true with our emotions and other felt needs. The apostle Paul tells us not to allow sin to reign in our mortal body or offer the parts of our body as instruments of wickedness, for sin should not be our master (see Romans 6).

The Discipline of Training

As we've already seen in the previous chapter, Paul didn't merely restrict his body, he trained it. People can be well educated but not well trained. As believers, happiness is found when we thrive in our new natures, not by indulging our old ones. The discipline of training is necessary in order to acquire the skills of a happy and holy life. Training goes into the very depth of your being—it is how you are, without having to give it a whole lot of thought. For example, the well-trained athlete or musician responds in the very fibers of their muscles when he or she is performing, not in their brain.

As children, we were trained to eat food with silverware instead of our hands, to use the toilet instead of soiling our britches, to wash ourselves when we notice we smell bad, and to brush our teeth when we get up and before we go to bed. We don't think about doing those things anymore, our body just does them and would feel bad if we didn't. Training in basic hygiene and self-care is crucial. It gives a child good habits in which to function in our society. If he or she refused these basics, they would be odd and become social outcasts.

In addition to training in personal hygiene, we need biblical training in moral, social, relational, emotional, and spiritual development as well. For example, no one teaches a child to lie, but they have to be trained to tell the truth. No one shows a child how to have a temper tantrum or to be selfish, but parents have to train their children to obey, to share, and to express their negative emotions constructively. Children don't develop maturity overnight and neither do Christians. It takes years of consistent training and repetitive practice by parents, teachers, coaches, pastors, and other influencers to teach children basic manners, how to problem solve, to get along with others, how to have constructive conflict, and even how to think and reason effectively. As believers we need to stop being impatient with the process, but we do need to train if we want to be beautiful and happy.

Training in Righteousness

We've covered much of this aspect of training in the previous chapter on becoming more beautiful. There are many well-written books on how to train in righteousness but these spiritual disciplines are best practiced in a community of others that can correct, instruct, pray for, and encourage you, which is a function of the local church body. Just as a child is not going to mature properly without being in a family, we cannot mature without the family of God.

Those who train to develop or enhance a particular skill, work harder and do more when they participate in groups. For example, professional athletes don't train all by themselves. He or she has a coach, a personal trainer, and a team that they work with. I know that when

I exercise alone, I am less likely to push myself to a harder level than when I'm doing it in a class or working with a trainer. I encourage you to get involved in a small group or Sunday school class and seek a spiritual mentor and/or accountability person who can help you train yourself to be more beautiful.

Remember, training in righteousness is learning to surrender our will to God. It's teaching our senses to take joy in what is good and to feel disgusted with everything evil (Romans 12:9). We are training our heart, mind, and will to prefer and pursue light over darkness, love over hate, justice over oppression, humility over pride, selflessness over selfishness, beauty rather than ugliness. The Bible says of itself, "All Scripture is God-breathed and is useful for teaching, rebuking, correcting and *training in righteousness,* so that the man of God may be thoroughly equipped for every good work" (2 Timothy 3:16-17).

Discipline of Attentiveness

Have you ever driven a long, boring stretch of highway and all of a sudden become aware that you have no idea where you are? Your body took over while your conscious mind wandered elsewhere and you've still managed to drive successfully for a period of time but have no memory of it. Now you worry, *Did I miss my exit? Where exactly am I? How long have I been driving in this trance?*

There are people who go through much of their life on automatic pilot. They aren't paying attention to themselves and what is happening around them. They function seemingly awake but with little inner awareness of how they think, feel, what motivates them, or what truly makes them happy. They do what they've always done without reflecting on why it's not working for them. When they feel unhappy, they believe they are helpless to change anything. They blame life, God, or other people for their unhappiness. They want change, but it's not up to them. They are unaware of their contribution to the problem or their responsibility for the solution.

Throughout the Scriptures, we are encouraged to do things that help us remember the truth and be attentive to the larger spiritual realities present:

- The writer of Hebrews warned, "We must pay more careful attention...to what we have heard, so that we do not drift away" (Hebrews 2:1).

- We are to take the time to reflect and think about what we are doing and why we're doing it (Haggai 1:7).

- Paul teaches us to examine ourselves to see if we are living what we say we believe (2 Corinthians 13:5), so that we don't deceive ourselves (1 John 1:8), which is our natural inclination (Jeremiah 17:9; Romans 1:25).

- Paul also instructs us to examine ourselves before we partake in communion, for example, so that we do not participate in this important celebration on automatic pilot, without awareness and appreciation of all God has done (1 Corinthians 11:28).

Stan, one of my clients said, "I get so caught up in the temporal part of life, I need to learn to pay more attention." We must train ourselves to see ourselves truthfully and to take responsibility for the changes that we need to make. Recently another one of my clients said to me, "I've become aware that I'm avoiding and hiding from things I know I need to implement in my life." For her and Stan, these moments of awareness became the beginning of significant change. Remember, we can't change something we do not see.

We talked earlier in chapter 4 about blind spots and the dangers they pose. The discipline of awareness and attentiveness doesn't diminish all of our blind spots, but it helps us to be more mindful that we have them. In that way, we become more aware of our shortcomings and faults. We don't think we know more than we do, or that we're better than we are. We're more open to correction and instruction, and we're cognizant of the fact that we might not be seeing everything as it really is.

A big part of training in righteousness not only involves growing in our awareness of ourselves and building our spiritual strengths, but also gaining a greater attentiveness toward God himself. Contemporary believers are hungering for an encounter with the living, loving, beautiful God. We need more presence, and that is only possible when we are attentive to him.

Even those who knew Jesus while he lived on earth didn't always recognize who he was. Their eyes were blinded, their hearts dull. Blaise Pascal believed that

> the greatest enemy, not only of prayer but also of the whole spiritual life of man, was inattention, drowsiness, complacency, what he called "the Gethsemane Sleep," referring to what the Apostles did when Jesus asked them to watch with him.[4]

Happiness is being fully alive, awake, and attentive to the awe and beauty of God. It washes over us when we pause to notice a beautiful sunset or inhale a fragrant flower. Love sneaks up on us when we wait quietly in his presence, and our heart leaps for joy when we hear his still small voice whisper to us. We find joy and a sense of purpose when we partner with God and help the poor, the needy, the lost, and those who have no voice to be heard.

Happiness is finding God, and in finding God, you find yourself.

Attentiveness Applied

I want to give you something specific you can do to practice becoming more attentive and aware. One discipline that I find particularly helpful is planning periods of time for silence and solitude. We live in such a noisy, busy world. Cell phones, text messages, and e-mails are constantly beckoning for our immediate attention, not to mention real people and endless chores and responsibilities. It's easy to become overwhelmed and shut down to all but the next thing. It's a horrible way to exist, but many of us live at that pace day in and day out without a moment for quiet reflection to enjoy his creation, or to listen for God's still small voice.

Training to become more attentive and aware means that you create a space for enough quiet in your outer life so that you can hear what's going on in your inner life. What rises to the surface when you aren't distracted with e-mails, phone calls, text messages, or endless jobs to be done? Sometimes we become aware of things that we didn't know about ourselves. When the whirling around us settles, we often see more clearly who we are, what we want, what's important to us, what we love, what we hate, what makes our soul sing, and what sucks us dry. We discover that we're happiest watching the birds flutter at our feeder and taking long walks by the stream, but we've been so used to our hectic pace, we don't actually take the time to do it.

Could you give yourself ten minutes a day or dedicate one hour a week for solitude and silence? As you become comfortable with the practice try to extend it to one day a month. You may even want to dedicate one weekend a year to do nothing and talk to no one but God.

· · · · · · · · · · **Expanding the Heart** · · · · · · · · ·

Ruth Haley Barton wrote about her own journey of becoming more aware and attentive to her heart's longings. She wrote,

> I have learned that the practices of solitude and silence are not merely self-indulgent exercises for those times when an overcrowded soul needs a little time to itself. Rather, they are concrete ways of opening to the presence of God beyond human effort and beyond the human constructs that cannot fully contain Divine Reality.[5]

· ·

We all need more awareness of ourselves, more awareness of God, and more awareness of God in us and God for us. This is the path to experiencing joy.

Man's Great End

LORD OF ALL BEING,
There is one thing that deserves my greatest care,
    that calls forth my ardent desires,
That is, that I may answer the great end for which I am made—
    to glorify thee who has given me being,
    and to do all the good I can for my fellow men;
Verily life is not worth having
    if it be not improved for this noble purpose.
Yet, Lord, how little is this the thought of mankind!
Most men seem to live for themselves,
    without much or any regard for thy glory,
    or for the good of others;
They earnestly desire and eagerly pursue
    the riches, honours, pleasures of this life,
    as if they supposed that wealth, greatness, merriment,
    could make their immortal souls happy;
But, alas, what false delusive dreams are these!
And how miserable ere long will those be that sleep in them,
    for all our happiness consists in loving thee,
And being holy as thou art holy.

O may I never fall into the tempers and vanities,
    of the sensuality and folly of the present world!
It is a place of inexpressible sorrow, a vast empty nothingness;
Time is a moment, a vapour,
    and all its enjoyments are empty bubbles,
    fleeting blasts of wind,

from which nothing satisfactory can be derived;
Give me grace always to keep in covenant with thee,
    and to reject as delusion a great name here or hereafter,
    together with all sinful pleasures or profits.
Help me to know continually
    that there can be no true happiness,
    no fulfilling of thy purpose for me,
Apart from a life lived in and for the Son of thy love.[6]

Questions for
• • • • • •
Thought and Discussion

1. Psychiatrist Scott Peck, author of *The Road Less Traveled,* observed that one of the main impediments to growth is laziness.[7] How has laziness contributed to your unhappiness and lack of growth as a person and as a Christian?

2. François Fenelon writes, "A persuaded mind and even a well intentioned heart is a long way from exact and faithful practice."[8] How have you found this to be true in your own life? What discipline can you begin to specifically implement in your life to get you where you want to go?

3. Christian counselor and author Ed Welch, PhD, says, "True humanness is, to our surprise, not about giving in to temptation. Instead, we are created to say no to both Satan's devices and our own desires that oppose the character of God."[9] In what particular way could you practice the discipline of restraint to help you grow to be more beautiful?

4. Read Romans 8:2 and 2 Peter 1:3. How does the gospel both redeem us from the penalty of sin and the power of sin?

5. Reflect upon this statement: "We learn best by doing, not by thinking about doing." What does this have to do with training?

6. Read Genesis 28:16. Jacob wrestled with an angel and declared, "Surely the LORD is in this place, and I did not know it" (ESV). How could you begin to be more attentive to the presence of God in your life?

7. Leonard Sweet wrote, "Prayer is not what you do to get God's attention. Prayer is what you do to bring yourself to attend to God and to pay attention to others."[10] Name something specific you are willing to start in order to better attend to God and to others.

8. Reflect upon this statement: "Being fully human takes practice. Without training we live a degraded life." Imagine what a child would look like with no training in hygiene or social skills. What about a Christian who has never trained themselves in godliness?

9. Summarize the benefits of discipline. Read Proverbs 8:32-36, 1 Corinthians 9:25, Luke 6:40, and Hebrews 5:14. Recall some of the consequences of not disciplining yourself from this chapter (review Proverbs 12:1; 5:21,23; 15:32; and Titus 2:11-12).

10. It's important to be attentive to the choices we make. Would you rather live with the pain of discipline or the pain of regret?

PART THREE

Practicing Happiness

Chapter 9

The Intentional Life

*I feel, I feel like one who has had his violin out of tune with the
orchestra and at last is in harmony with the music of the universe.*

FRANK LAUBACH

*We seldom realize fully that we are sent to fulfill God-given tasks.
We act as if we were simply dropped down in creation and have
to decide to entertain ourselves until we die. But we were sent into
the world by God, just as Jesus was. Once we start living our lives
with that conviction, we will soon know what we were sent to do.*

HENRI J.M. NOUWEN

WHEN MY CHILDREN WERE YOUNG, they attended a small private Christian school. The annual Christmas concert was eagerly anticipated and equally dreaded. We loved to see our little darlings in their angel costumes singing their hearts out, even if sometimes they sang a little off key. But the band and orchestra was a different experience—at least for those of us who had no children participating. When the music began, the children tried hard but there was no discernable melody and everyone played their individual instrument to their own rhythm, as loudly as they could. During one song, I closed my eyes for a minute and joked with my husband that if I didn't know better, I'd think I was in the middle of a noisy New York City traffic jam.

More recently, my husband and I attended a banquet where our local high school orchestra performed as the featured entertainment. We were astonished to hear such beautiful music from these talented teenagers. It was obvious that they had spent many hours practicing and memorizing their songs. Before they began playing, each musician paused and focused his or her attention on the concert master in order to tune the instrument with hers. The musicians each had their own part, but never strove to be heard individually. Together they made beautiful music. Occasionally, a musician would notice that his or her instrument fell slightly off pitch. When that happened, he or she simply paused to re-tune.

In a similar fashion, God has given us each our own unique instrument, which is our body, embedded with talents, skills, and personality, to develop and use for his purposes. His desire is for human beings to have meaningful work that blesses our planet, helps and enriches others, and brings him glory. The apostle Paul says, "We are God's workmanship, created in Christ Jesus to do good works, which God prepared in advance for us to do" (Ephesians 2:10) We live as we were created only when we stay in tune with God.

Each of us has something to do in God's kingdom. When we live from our purpose, we will feel more alive and in tune than if we simply sleepwalk through each day doing whatever comes next without any plan or reflection as to who we are, why God made us, and for what purpose.

First, let us look at living *on purpose* and how we can live more intentionally. Next, we'll learn how to live *with purpose* and why that is important if we want to be happy.

Living on Purpose

What comes to mind when we think about living on purpose? Children often say, "I didn't do it on purpose." Meaning, "I didn't intend for this to happen." Living on purpose indicates we do intend some things to happen. We set goals, we make plans, we know where we want to go, and we are working toward getting there. We can spend the same amount of time, energy, and fuel, driving around in circles as we can to travel to a preplanned destination. If we want to live intentionally, we must ask ourselves what it is that we want and what's important to us. Do our days have a direction, goals, and a purpose, or are we merely busy with a lot of activities but in essence, wandering around in circles?

As I was writing this book, I'd ask people to fill in the blank: "If only I had more _____, then I'd be happy." Besides *money,* one of the most frequent answers people gave was *time. If only I had more time, then I'd be happy.* We need more time like we need more storage space. Organizing our living space has become a thriving business because we buy stuff we believe we need and think will make us happy. But whatever it was, we don't use it any longer and now it's just cluttering up our space. Consequently, we need more places to put all the stuff we don't need or use anymore but don't want to throw or give away. If you think more time will help you, what do you need more time for? Are you currently using the 24 hours you're given each day wisely?

The psalmist prays, "Teach us to number our days aright, that we may gain a heart of wisdom" (Psalm 90:12). Paul instructs us to "be very careful, then, how you live—not as unwise but as wise, making the most of every opportunity, because the days are evil" (Ephesians 5:15). In her book *The How of Happiness,* Sonja Lyubomirsky says, "In a nutshell, the fountain of happiness can be found in how you behave, what you think, and what goals you set every day of your life."[1]

We don't necessarily need more time, but to spend our time living our lives more purposefully. Let's look at some ways to do that.

Slow Down

If we want to live on purpose and not merely be busy, we will need to first stop hurrying in order to see clearly. When you spin an object, such as the blades of a fan, fast enough, it gives you the illusion of something solid, something permanent. Only when you slow it down do you see it for what it really is. Many of us spin our lives faster and faster, doing more, striving harder, hoping that if we're busy enough, it must mean that we matter, our life has meaning, or we are important.

We need to see chronic busyness as a warning bell that we've gotten out of tune with God and reduced ourselves into *human doings* instead of human beings. Doing things is important but they do not define who we are as persons. In fact many times we use our job title or role to identify ourselves and allow it to define our worth and value. For example, we say, "I am a counselor, or pastor, a teacher, or secretary, or I'm just a mom." Our roles or titles describe what we do, not how well we do it, nor who we are.

In our culture, we have identified our own worth and one another's value by external factors such as possessions, performance, power, or popularity. We've worn busyness as a badge of honor and virtue, even among believers. People often say, "I don't know how you do it all," or "Wow, you must really be busy doing God's work." Meaning you must be close to God or very disciplined. When I am clear-minded and in tune with God, I think to myself, *Don't be fooled. Chronic busyness is nothing more than a false sense of your own importance, not a mark of true spirituality.*

We need to ask ourselves and one another not, *How do you do it all?* but, *Why are you doing what you're doing?* If we want to live on purpose, we must question not only why we are doing stupid or foolish things, but probably more crucial, why we are doing *good* things. What drives a woman to be the president of the PTA, the carpool mom, and the neighborhood babysitter? Do these activities fit in with who she is and her life goals and purpose? Why am I speaking all over the place or writing books? What's the reason I jam my schedule so full of counseling appointments that sometimes I don't have time to eat dinner? I've asked myself, *Is it really to serve God, or am I trying to find my significance out of what I do?* Jesus did many wonderful things, but he never rushed or seemed too busy for what really mattered. His life was lived on purpose and with purpose. Busyness, even with good things, is never a substitute for a close relationship with God or godly character, nor will it ever lead to happiness.

Slowing down creates precious time to tune ourselves into God's love, his purposes, and to practice his presence. Instead of frantic activity with its side effects of exhaustion, crabbiness, and/or burnout, we come to see that we don't have to play every song that's requested or need to master every piece in the orchestra, nor is God asking us to do so. God always prioritizes who we are becoming over what particular activities we do.

I am learning, and I hope you are too, that it is not all up to us, neither is it all about us. Our whole world will not collapse if we slow down, take a day off, or eliminate some things from our schedule.

Engage in Meaningful Rest and Smart Recreation

Experiencing pleasure is an important part of feeling happy. It is not wrong, sinful, or selfish to enjoy your life and take time out to play—in fact, it's crucial to your well-being and happiness. Unfortunately many of us spend whatever relaxing time we allow ourselves indulging in meaningless and even harmful activities, such as mindless shopping, watching too much television, playing hours of games on the computer, Internet gambling, hanging out in chat rooms, or viewing pornography, to mention a few.

God instituted the Sabbath so that we would have a day each week to intentionally slow down, do nothing, be quiet, and rest. I used to see this as legalistic and boring, but I have come to treasure doing nothing on purpose. We need to turn off sometimes in order to recharge. For many people there is no distinct time during their week where they choose to stop their normal busy routine.

Living on purpose does not imply that you have to be productive and work all the time, quite the contrary. It means that you plan time to refresh your body, soul, spirit, as well as your relationships in smart ways. Take a day or even an hour and turn off the television, computer, washing machine, DVD player, and cell phone and see what happens. Instead of surfing the web or channel cruising, choose to take a walk in the park with a loved one, invite company for dinner and just play board games and talk. Learn to cultivate a garden or sit and watch the birds. Initially you might feel bored or even a little anxious because our brains have been used to being overstimulated with gadgets and activities, so much so that some of us feel deadened, not happy.[2]

When you are purposeful in creating meaningful recreation and enjoy life in good ways, you will find yourself renewed, happier, and have fresh enthusiasm about what you do as well as greater clarity about what your values and purposes are.

Invest in Yourself

Although we share many characteristics common to our humanity, each of us also has special gifts as well as limitations that help shape our life's mission. For example, I was not given any special abilities or affections for math or science. Quite the opposite, I always preferred the humanities. I love to read and talk with people, not work with gadgets or numbers.

Knowing myself helped me focus on a direction for my life and how to use my passions and strengths to discover my particular bent. Living on purpose means that we pay attention to what talents, gifts, and abilities God has put inside us and diligently work to cultivate them. The apostle Paul instructed young Timothy to fan into flames the gifts God had given him (2 Timothy 1:6). Each of us possesses raw talents and unique gifts that improve with focused effort.

The high school musicians that played beautiful music were naturally gifted, but every one of them diligently practiced to mature their God-given talent. Perhaps even some of them started in that elementary orchestra at my children's school. A talented athlete, musician, or artist isn't born being proficient in their area of expertise; they work at it through disciplined training and practice.

Tammy, a successful corporate attorney, was asked to speak to a woman in her church whose husband was abusive. After hearing some of the heartbreaking stories of women who were not represented fairly in court, her heart was burdened with the injustice of the legal system toward women. She decided to leave her cushy job to start a law practice that served these kinds of clients. She made less money but was a lot happier. Tammy allowed God to use her unique gifts and training to help others, thus fulfilling his purposes for her.

• •

A question people always ask me is, "How do I know God's telling me to do something, and it's not just me who wants it?" I encourage them to follow his leading *and* their heart's desires. In *A Testament of Devotion,* Quaker Thomas Kelly writes,

> But the Loving Presence does not burden us equally with all things, but considerately puts upon each of us just a few central tasks, as emphatic responsibilities. For each of us these special undertakings are our share in the joyous burdens of love.
>
> Thus the state of having a concern has a foreground and a background. In the foreground is the special task, uniquely illuminated toward which we feel a special yearning and care...But in the background is a second level, or layer, or universal concern for all the good things that need doing. Toward them all we feel kindly, but we are dismissed from active service in most of them.[3]

God is not dependent upon us to accomplish his intentions in the world but he gives us the privilege of participating in work of eternal significance. Sadly, many people don't pay enough attention to crafting and maturing their own personal instrument or discovering what songs we are uniquely designed to play by listening to their heart's dreams and desires. We're not even in tune with ourselves or our Creator much of the time. Instead, we toot our own horn in our own timing without any thought to the kind of song we could be learning or have been called to play.

Every person has been given an instrument but they're not all the same. You may not be an attorney or even college educated, but please don't minimize your contribution to the overall music just because your instrument isn't fancy or you aren't a soloist. What would a concerto sound like with all violins? An orchestra needs tubas and oboes, tambourines and bassoons. Playing melodies and harmonies in tune with other instruments creates music. This is the picture of the body of Christ and the church working together to glorify God. When we are out of tune and out of sync with one another, and the conductor, all we hear is noise. (See 1 Corinthians 12:12-31 for more of Paul's teaching on this subject.)

Stay Awake, Keep Alert

Ironically Peter, the disciple who thought he was more courageous than he really was and who fell asleep in the garden, is the one who warns us about mental and spiritual dullness. He says, "Be self-controlled and alert. Your enemy the devil prowls around like a roaring lion looking for someone to devour" (1 Peter 5:8). Don't let it be you.

Mary came to counseling with mild depression and, as she reported, "poor self-esteem." Long before her depression set in, Mary habitually spent much of her day playing games on her computer and watching home shopping channels and reality shows on television. Her house was a mess and her children were neglected. Mary seemed clueless that her bad habits were contributing to her current state of mind. She saw her depression as something that happened to her, not as the result of her lifestyle choices. Her depression was actually a gift that helped her wake up and realize that something was dreadfully wrong. She needed to pay attention so that she could learn to live on purpose instead of merely exist.

First, I helped Mary choose some simple goals. She said she wanted to get her home in order and spend more quality time with her children. To actually accomplish those goals she needed to discipline herself to turn off the distractions that were robbing her of her real life.

She didn't change these habits all at once, but she began with short 15 minute intervals three or four times a day. She would wash her dishes, or put dinner in the Crock-Pot, help her children with their homework, or take a walk. I asked her to pay attention to how she felt about her life, herself, and her family afterward. Mary noticed that when she lived her life awake and intentional rather than lazily sleepwalking through her day, she felt better and her self-esteem improved. That motivated her to continue making positive changes and she felt happier.

Like Mary did, we may live haphazardly, recklessly, selfishly, lazily, or sinfully. We're asleep to what really matters, or we are so busy chasing what we think will make us happy, we are wasting our lives. Sometimes we spend more time reading up on or watching the escapades of famous people or movie stars than we do cultivating a meaningful life of our own. We're out of sync with our Creator and our created purpose and we don't even know it.

Living a life on purpose starts by being aware that you have choices every day and that those choices have consequences and those consequences affect many things including your happiness levels. As Moses instructed the Israelites before entering the Promised Land, choose life!

Living with Purpose

Living *on* purpose helps us to clarify what's good, what's true, and what's important so that we can live each day *with* purpose instead of meaninglessness. Some of us have found our life purposes and are living on purpose. We're working to develop our gifts but we still may be doing too much. How will we know? We're not happy. We feel physically and emotionally drained, overwhelmed, stressed, burned out, or depressed. It's time to slow down, create more balance, and have more fun in our lives.

For others, it can be very stressful discerning one's life purpose. They don't know what direction they should go or what specifically they are to *do*. Even when they are intentional about living on purpose, they still lack a sense of living with purpose and as a result, feel anxious instead of peaceful or restless instead of happy. If that's where you're at, I want you to start implementing these next steps. They will help you live with purpose in your daily life, even if you haven't figured out what your particular gifts and calling are.

Simplify

I've been thinking about redecorating my kitchen and bathroom for some time but I'm overwhelmed with the choices. Picking out new wallpaper, paint colors, and different hardware has turned into a full-time job. Life has gotten very complicated when making even simple choices feels stressful because there are thousands of options to choose from.

One of my friends wrote me recently and said,

> As I've been thinking of what would make me, and others I know happier, the word *simplify* stands out in my mind. In our world of excess, insatiable appetites, decadence, constant busyness (the list could go on) it feels like an overcrowded room without space to think, move, or breathe. It is suffocating…squeezing the happiness right out of my life.

Paul prayed that we would be able to discern what is best so that we would be filled with the fruit of righteousness (Philippians 1:9-11). Simplifying our life choices teaches us to clarify the difference between what's good and what's best. Good things, like ministry, serving on committees, a great job or career, taking care of a house, or even helping the homeless, are wonderful, but they can become the subtle enemy of the best things if your love for doing them is out of order. Simplifying doesn't mean that we give up everything that's meaningful to us, but it means that we will discern the things that truly matter, put other responsibilities or activities in their rightful place, and let go of the rest.

When God tells us to choose life, he doesn't make it complicated. He tells us what the most important and best choices are. Jesus said all the commandments can be summed up into two. Love God first and love others well. When that becomes primary, you *are* living on purpose and with purpose and everything else you do falls into its proper place.

Make God Famous

Sophie attended a woman's conference where I was speaking and asked me afterwards if she could talk with me. Obviously distraught, she had no idea what she was supposed to *do* with her life. She was a single girl with some obvious psychological/emotional limitations. Before coming to Christ, she had been in and out of mental hospitals. Currently she couldn't find a job, she wasn't equipped to go to school, and consequently she felt like a lump of flesh that served no good purpose.

My heart went out to her. I held her hands and said, "Sophie, I disagree. You *do* have a purpose and important work to do. God will use you, but it will be within the context of your life story, with your strengths as well as your limitations. God doesn't waste our life experiences or our suffering. He uses them if we're willing. He wants *you* to make him famous."

Surprised, Sophie asked, "How can I make God famous? I have no skills."

I told her, "I think we have made living with purpose too complicated at times. The apostle Paul explains God's will rather simply. He says that it is God's will that we mature and live a holy life. (See 1 Thessalonians 4:3-7.) With God's help, Sophie, you can do that even if you never hold down a regular job. Jesus said that they will know we are Christians by our love for one another" (John 13:34-35).

Tears welled up in Sophie's eyes.

"Sophie," I said, "that is living with purpose. It isn't more complicated than that." I added, "Sophie, God has given you important work to do. You have the privilege and responsibility to make God famous to individuals that only you will know. You will be able to love people that only you come in contact with. When they see your newfound joy and the sparkle in your eyes, they will ask you the reason for the hope that is in you (1 Peter 3:15). Others may ask you, 'How can you trust God is good when you've suffered so much?' Or 'How can you forgive your parents for neglecting you when you were smaller?' Or 'How can you still be joyful with all your struggles?' You will have the opportunity to tell them about Jesus and his love, mercy, and grace for you."

The road that God takes us on to accomplish those purposes is different for each of us, but wherever we are and whatever we do, God's desire is that we grow up and love others well so that we will reflect Christlikeness in our lives (Romans 8:29). He wants others to look at us and wonder what makes us different. Where do we get our patience, our strength, our peace, our joy, and our happiness even in the midst of hardships?

> Dr. Francis Collins is one of the leading geneticists in the world. As a non-believer, he was intrigued by the peace and faith of Christians who went through seemingly unbearable suffering. With his interest piqued in spiritual things, Dr. Collins decided to investigate the evidence for the existence of God. After a thorough consideration of the evidence, he became a believer. While the evidence convinced his mind,

the hope of the suffering believers attracted his heart. God used the suffering of Christians to draw this brilliant scientist to Himself.[4]

Sophie isn't finished maturing (as none of us are), but just as we are and right where we are, people are watching our lives. Jesus said that we are the light of the world (Matthew 5:14). To live with purpose is to be aware that we can reflect Christ in such a way that broken and hurting people are drawn to him like moths to light.

Nurture Your Relationships

We live in a busy world that prioritizes getting things done over nurturing intimate connection. Even in church, people feel lonely and neglected. We forget that what we don't maintain deteriorates. An untended garden soon becomes overgrown with weeds. Our homes need upkeep, our cars need regular oil changes, our bodies need to be washed, our hair combed, and nails trimmed, or we will soon look ragged. Why is it that we think that somehow our relationships will maintain themselves and don't have to be refreshed or repaired?

When we live with purpose, we understand that most of our maturing process is learning how to love people well. Our human love is a need-based love and usually deteriorates into an unloving me-first, selfish love. During relationship struggles, I often hear individuals say, "What's in it for me?" or "I'm not happy—I'm not getting anything out of this relationship," or "What about my needs?"

Living with purpose doesn't mean we must connect meaningfully with everyone. Jesus didn't. He couldn't. He was limited by his humanness as we are. But it does mean that we intentionally invest in those people God has put in our lives and we do what we can to love well and pursue reconciliation and peace when there is a relational speed bump or detour.[5]

The simplest thing you can do to invest in your relationship is to give it the gift of unstructured time. When my children were young, parenting experts said that quality time was more important than the quantity of time. Although there is a grain of truth to that, you cannot create meaningful moments on demand. You must simply be present often enough to catch them when they happen and enjoy them. Give your time to people just because you want to be with them, not just because you have to, or are supposed to, or you need them to get something for yourself.

Studies have shown that those who have loving connections and strong relationships are happier than those who don't. They are also better able to handle stress and traumatic life events.[6] As a Jewish proverb says, "Sticks in a bundle are not easily broken, sticks alone can be broken by a child."

Do Justice, Love Mercy

The Old Testament prophet Micah told God's people what God required for a life well-lived. He said, "He has showed you, O man, what is good. And what does the LORD require of you? To act justly and to love mercy and to walk humbly with your God" (Micah 6:8).

Throughout the Scriptures God calls his people to help the needy, care for the poor, to give a voice to those who are powerless, stand up for injustice, and stand against evil. What usually makes us most angry is not what breaks the heart of God, but not getting our own needs met. Instead, what ought to make us angry are children sold into sex slavery, women abandoned by husbands or ones that are abused by them. What ought to break our heart is the ethnic cleansing in Africa and those unfairly imprisoned and persecuted for their faith. We spend a fortune on cosmetic surgery, our pets, and gardens, but the local church struggles to pay its pastor, and missionaries are coming home from the field because they lack adequate resources and support. Children are starving throughout the world and Americans are struggling with obesity.

We are missing Jesus' message on what makes an abundant life. It is not about us living the good life, but it is God's plan to use us to help a broken, battered, and dying world. I received a Christmas card from Covenant House many years ago. I was so convicted I framed it and keep it on my shelf above my desk. This is what it said.

> On the street I saw a small girl
> cold and shivering in a thin dress,
> with little hope of a decent meal.
> I became angry and said to God:
> "Why did you permit this?
>   Why don't you do
>   something about it?"
>
> For a while God said nothing.
> That night He replied
> quite suddenly:
> "I certainly did something about it—
>   I made you.'"

What specific places, persons, or causes has God uniquely equipped you to give your resources of time, energy, gifting, and money to? Secular research studies evaluating the happiness levels of students helping others versus going out and having a good time reveal that helping others results in feeling happier for a longer period time.[7] Jesus was right—it is more blessed to give than receive (Acts 20:35).

Live Fully in the Moment

Unhappy people are often living in yesterday or wishing for tomorrow. They keep putting off their purpose and their happiness until they get all their ducks lined up in a row. This moment is all you have so make it count.

Yesterday, I returned from a speaking engagement in California through the Philadelphia airport. This isn't my first choice, not only because this airport isn't the closest one to my home, but also because it always takes a long time getting from the airport to the long-term parking lot. Despite what they advertise, the shuttle bus does not run as frequently as they say, and sometimes it is too full to pick up new passengers. Hauling my luggage up on the bus is always a hassle, especially after a long trip. Tired and crabby passengers are the norm.

The shuttle pulled to the curb and for the first time in my airport experience, the driver got out and helped people with their suitcases. He was kind, cheerful, and funny. During the drive to the long-term lot, he provided us with helpful information about how to find our car if we forgot where we parked or didn't know our license plate numbers. I've been traveling through this airport for years and had never heard these tips. I observed his effect on the rest of us riding. People smiled. They became friendlier toward one another, and helped one another get their luggage off the shuttle.

This bus driver loved his work and it showed. He was in *flow,* a term psychologist Mihaly Csikszentmihalyi coined to define "a state in which one is immersed in an experience that is rewarding in and of itself, a state in which we feel we are one with the experience, in which 'action and awareness are merged.'"[8] In that short drive from the terminal to the parking lot, that shuttle driver made a difference in my day. Others felt it too. He was happy and it was contagious. The apostle Paul says, "Whatever you do, do it all for the glory of God" (1 Corinthians 10:31). You can wash the dishes, wipe a runny nose, or type a memo, with flow. We don't have to do great things to live with purpose. Mother Teresa once said, "We just need to do little things, with great love."

🌀

The writer of Ecclesiastes was busy, important, rich, popular, and powerful, but at the end, as we have learned, he declared his life was nothing but smoke. As he reflected back, he clarified and simplified how to live on purpose and with purpose. Let's look at what he said,

Take care of yourself, have a good time, and make the
most of whatever job you have for as long as God gives
you life...

Seize life! Eat bread with gusto. Drink wine with a
robust heart. Oh yes—God takes pleasure in *your* pleasure!
Relish life with the spouse you love each and every day of
your precarious life. Each day is God's gift...

Be generous; Invest in acts of charity. Charity yields high
returns. Don't hoard your goods; spread them around. Be
a blessing to others. This could be your last night...Don't
stare at the clouds. Get on with your life.

Don't take a single day for granted. Take delight in
each light-filled hour, remembering that there will also be
many dark days and that most of what comes your way
is smoke...

Fear God. Do what he tells you (Ecclesiastes 5:18; 9:7-9:
11:1-2,4,8; 12:13 MSG).

Live like it matters, because it does.

Questions for
Thought and Discussion

1. Reflect on how you spend your time, talents, and energy. Is it on
purpose and with purpose? What has stood out to you that will
help you be more intentional?

2. Describe your typical leisure time. Is it directed toward refreshment, or is it mindless or even destructive?

3. Jan Johnson writes, "Our problem is not lack of time, but failure to value the moment and to see God at work in it."[9] How can you be more intentional about valuing each moment and looking for God in the midst of it?

4. What specific steps can you take this next week to make more space for quiet and for God? When you do get quiet, what do you notice?

5. How have you invested in developing your God-given talents and abilities? Thinking about them may begin to help you see how God has uniquely designed you and how you can develop the gifts he has given you to become your best self.

Here are some Web sites where you can take online tests to discover your personal strengths as well as spiritual gifts.

- *www.authentichappiness.org.* This is a secular site on positive psychology. It provides a number of tests you can take, such as assessing your signature strengths, measuring your current happiness levels, and others.

- *http://www.Christianet.com/bible/spiritualgiftstest.htm.* This is a test to evaluate which are your strongest spiritual gifts
- *www.Churchgrowth.org/cgi-cg/gifts.cgi?intro=1.* This is a similar test on spiritual gifting, with a slightly different slant in that it focuses more on working within a church or team and how you might best fit in.
- *www.discoveryourpersonality.com.* This site gives you various time-tested personality and career tests you can take. There is a charge for taking the tests and getting an analysis of the results, but if you have no idea as to what your God-given bent is, they may be helpful.

6. The author says that relationships need to be maintained, refreshed, and repaired. What kind of investment are you making in your relationships? Have you been intentional about nurturing those connections? What changes do you need to make to improve and enhance your personal relationships?

7. Read 1 Peter 2:9. Name one way we make God famous.

8. George Bernard Shaw wrote,

   This is the true joy in life, the being used for a purpose recognized by yourself as a mighty one; the being thoroughly worn out before you are thrown on the scrap heap; the being a force of Nature instead of a feverish selfish little clog of ailments and grievances complaining that the world will not devote itself to making you happy.[10]

Do you agree or disagree? What steps can you begin to take to make your life more intentionally useful to God's purposes?

9. Read Isaiah 1:17 and James 1:27. Living with purpose means that you are aware that God's plan to help others is you. What specific thing can you begin to do to live with that purpose in mind? How do you feel when you know God used you to help another person?

10. Read Deuteronomy 4:9. What steps can you take to help yourself not forget what God is teaching you?

CHAPTER 10

Making Lemonade

*We deem those happy who from the experience of life have
learned to bear its ills, without being overcome by them.*

JUVENAL

*Sweet are the uses of adversity,
Which like the toad, ugly and venomous,
Wears yet a precious jewel in his head.*

SHAKESPEARE

FOUR-YEAR-OLD ALEXANDRA "ALEX" SCOTT, diagnosed with cancer, made up
her mind that she wanted to raise money to help her doctors find a
cure for kids with cancer. With her brother's help, she set up a lemonade stand on their front lawn in July 2000. Despite her deteriorating
health, Alex continued her annual lemonade stand, inspiring thousands
of others to take up her cause. When little Alex died at age eight, she
had raised over one million dollars. Since her death in 2004, Alex's
Lemonade Stand Foundation has raised and donated millions of dollars toward finding a cure for childhood cancer.[1]

Alex literally took the lemons of her cancer diagnosis and made
lemonade. She used what most of us would see as a terrible tragedy
and turned it into a triumph and celebration of life as she worked to
raise funds to find a cure for children with cancer. None of us have

any guarantees that we won't receive some unwanted lemons during our lifetime. Therefore, it is crucial that we learn how to take the sour lemons life gives us and make sweet lemonade.

• • • • • • • • • • • **No Way Out?** • • • • • • • • • • • •

Christopher Reeve, producer, writer, and actor, more popularly known as Superman from the role he played in the movie, was paralyzed while horseback riding in 1995. His entire life changed. It would have been tempting to stay in the pit of despair and self-pity, but he, and his wife, Dana, did not. They started the Christopher and Dana Reeve Foundation and the Paralysis Resource Center which raises funds for research and promotes the health and well-being of people living with spinal-cord injuries. They were an inspiration for many who wondered how they could stay positive in the midst of such misfortune and suffering.

Joni Eareckson Tada, a beautiful woman inside and out, was paralyzed in a diving accident when she was only 17 years old. Throughout her life she has been an inspiration to thousands of people as she has turned her tragedy into a triumph of God's goodness and grace by starting a ministry to the disabled called Joni and Friends. Joni paints by holding the brush with her teeth, sings, speaks, and writes with a message that touches our soul with the reality of Christ. As a young woman she surely was tempted to stay in the pit of her depression and grief over her physical losses and limitations. She chose not to. Instead she allowed God to create beauty out of ashes.

In another situation, my former neighbor gave birth to a beautiful little girl with sparkling blue eyes, who was diagnosed with cerebral palsy. Her brain was as sharp as a tack but her body wouldn't cooperate. She was confined to a wheelchair, her speech difficult to understand. The thing I remember most about Emily, however, was her smile and her parents, who trusted God no matter what. They were teaching me how you turn lemons into lemonade.

• •

In chapter 3, we looked at how to get out of the pit of our habitual negative thoughts and emotions. But the pit isn't simply emotions, at least not at first. The pit is also our life circumstances when it seems that there is no way out.

For some of us, hardship hurtles toward us so fast it feels as if we will never recover. Our house burns down in a freak fire or a hurricane thrashes our neighborhood and nothing but rubble remains. Marriages break apart through death and divorce. Financial crisis, birth injuries or defects, job loss, health difficulties, sexual assault, and destructive and abusive relationships are part of this broken world. When such adversities become a part of our personal life, we feel scared, angry, hurt, sad, hopeless, and sometimes even depressed. We most definitely feel unhappy and often overwhelmed. We tell ourselves that we can't cope with it all—it feels too big. We question if we will ever feel happy again. Even if we wanted to, where would we start?

Start Where You Are

Please hear me. People experience great pain during these kinds of hardships, and I believe that "there is a time for breaking down," as the writer of Ecclesiastes said. Emily's parents grieved and asked "why" questions. I'm sure they pounded their fists and prayed. Joni went through a season of despair when she woke up paralyzed. When everything falls apart, the most helpful thing we can have is a strong network of supportive family and friends as well as a deep faith in a loving God. But even these things can get tested during adversity, and sometimes the people we thought were our close friends may disappear or fail us and others who we knew only casually now rally to our side in amazing ways. Hardship has a way of clarifying things as well as bringing people closer, and the bonds of genuine friendship tighten.

During times of suffering, not only do our relationships get tested but so does our faith. When life goes terribly wrong, most of us question God's love and doubt his goodness, at least a little. Like Job from the Old

Testament, we can't understand why he's allowed this to happen to us. Sooner or later we must wrestle with God and face our doubts in order to make some meaning of our suffering. This is a good thing and a way to start finding the ingredients to make lemonade out of life's lemons.

When the writer of Ecclesiastes wrote down his thoughts, he didn't end by saying there is "a time to break down," but he added that there is "a time to build up." He also wrote that there is "a time to weep, and a time to laugh; a time to mourn, and a time to dance; a time to cast away stones, and a time to gather stones together" (Ecclesiastes 3:3-5 ESV). Sometimes the worst of times also becomes the best of times. We begin to see life differently, develop closer friends, and learn important life lessons. Happiness isn't about feeling fabulous and never feeling pain. It's about feeling pain and finding purpose. It's about experiencing joy, hope, love, and peace in the midst of our tears.

Although for each person it may take a different amount of time, somewhere in our suffering we'll need to rise out of the rubble in order to cope with what's happened to us both internally and externally. This is where we have a say in what kind of story we are writing about our lives. We don't always understand that we play a very significant role in our own healing process. We can't always control what happens to us. But from this point on, if we want to mature and become holy and happy people, we must *decide* what we do with what happens to us. This is the most important part of our story. How we choose to respond to our adversity not only reveals our character, it shapes it.

Psychologists who study how people cope with traumatic life events provide overwhelming evidence that individuals who are somehow able to find the positive in the negative and work toward a solution, or extract some kind of meaning out of their tragedy do better physically, emotionally, and relationally, than those who aren't able to do these things.[2] You can choose to sit and do nothing, but studies have shown that people who squeeze whatever good they can out of their experience grow and become stronger, more resilient, and feel happier with themselves and life than those who don't.

Mining for Diamonds

One thing that helps us maintain a positive attitude even in a difficult situation is to actively look for meaning or purpose amidst the hard things. For some people this is easier said than done. Natural optimists can usually find the good in a situation. For pessimists, it's much more difficult. Mining for diamonds is hard, ugly work. They aren't easily seen embedded in the mud and muck of the earth. In the same way, God says that he gives us treasures in darkness but we really have to look for them (Isaiah 45:3). By discovering and, like Alex did with her lemonade stand, even creating good things in the middle of our trauma and trials, we can experience joy, peace, and purpose.

Sheila was not happy about being diagnosed with breast cancer, but once she started her chemotherapy, she realized that God had a purpose for her to be there. As she interacted with the doctors and nurses as well as with other patients during her treatments, she found herself cheering for them and encouraging their progress. Others would ask her, "How can you stay so positive in the midst of this terrible trial?" Sheila replied, "Cancer gave me a mission field and a mission. God gave me a job to do and it happened to be in the oncology ward." When Sheila saw her ordeal from that perspective, she found herself looking forward to her treatments and how God would use her. She found she could be happy even in the midst of her cancer.

While chained up in prison, the apostle Paul wrote,

> I want you to know, brothers, that what has happened to me has really served to advance the gospel. As a result, it has become clear throughout the whole palace guard and to everyone else that I am in chains for Christ. Because of my chains, most of the brothers in the Lord have been encouraged to speak the word of God more courageously and fearlessly (Philippians 1:12-13).

Paul never minimized suffering. He experienced enormous trials in his ministry and talked honestly about the pain of them, yet he didn't get stuck in the pit of despair. Looking for a higher purpose or meaning in his suffering helped Paul emotionally climb out. (Read 2 Corinthians 4:8-9 and 16-18 for an example.) Paul understood the power of our mental attitude on our emotional well-being, especially in difficult life circumstances.

If you are laboring to find meaning in a particularly difficult situation, try this exercise. Write about one of the most traumatic or difficult things you've ever gone through. Write for 15 minutes, for four consecutive days. But don't just vent. As you write, look to make sense of the causes and consequences of what happened. Every day dig a little deeper to extract the diamonds from the rubble. Write a new ending to an old story or close a chapter on an open wound. Let yourself see it in new ways.[3]

Look for the Benefits

For those of us committed to regular physical exercise, looking for the benefits is how we endure. Most folks I know don't enjoy exercise; it's painful, not fun. But what keeps people going is thinking about the results. They picture firm abs, lean legs, or a strong heart. In the same way, James reminds us that we can experience joy in the midst of our suffering when we know that God is using a difficult experience to build character muscles of endurance that will empower us to run the race of faith well (James 1:3).

When going through a difficult time, two questions we can ask ourselves that give us a recipe for lemonade are...

1. What strengths have I discovered in myself, or have the opportunity to develop?
2. What lessons have I learned?

The apostle Paul reminds us that, "We also rejoice in our sufferings, because we *know* that suffering produces perseverance; perseverance, character; and character, hope" (Romans 5:3-4).

What Strengths Do I Have or Can I Develop?

Susan lost her husband, John, in a terrible car accident. He was only 48 and left behind three teenagers. Susan and John were high school sweethearts, and when she was only 19, she had left her parents' home to marry John. She had never lived by herself, and she was not only grief-stricken, she was terrified.

Susan loved John deeply, but after he died she began to realize she had never fully grown up. John handled all the finances, made most of their decisions, and took care of everything regarding their house. Susan didn't know how to pay their bills online or even how to turn on their tractor or grass trimmer. How would she function without him to help her?

Not only was Susan alone, but she realized she was unprepared to handle her aloneness. Tempted to fall into despair, instead, she chose to embrace the changes. She learned many new skills, including how to pay her bills on the computer and how to turn on and ride the tractor.

Susan went to a financial counselor and made some decisions on what to do with John's life insurance. She began to get more involved in money management, took some courses, and even started an investment club for widows and divorced women. Susan discovered strengths she never knew she had but they came through the tragedy of John's unexpected death. Our attitude is often the only thing we can still control in a difficult or traumatic situation. When we stay positive and look for the good, we often discover unexpected blessings and opportunities that would have never happened had not this change entered our life.

Susan would never say she was happy John died, but she was finding that she could be a happy person again. She told me, "I am not the same woman I was a year ago. Not only have my life circumstances drastically changed, I've been transformed and that's been a good thing."

What Lessons Have I Learned?

Earlier, in chapter 3, Debbie was caught in the pit of her anger and hurt over Steve's infidelity. But as they worked on restoring their marriage, they both learned some powerful lessons. Debbie learned that she had been neglectful toward her husband and without realizing it, subtly demeaned him in front of others. This in no way justified Steve's affair, but it did cause Debbie to be aware of her contributions to the deterioration of their marriage. She realized that she had a part to play in Steve's vulnerabilities to the attention of another woman.

Steve learned that stuffing his feelings didn't make them go away and that the longer he ignored his hurt and anger, the more justified he felt in accepting the attentions of other women. He also learned that the grass isn't greener on the other side and that any good relationship takes work to maintain.

Neither of them would say they were happy about the affair, but both would say that they now have a happier marriage, feel closer to God and feel happier with themselves, with each other, and with life.

Even when things don't have a happy ending, there are still great lessons to extract from life's most difficult times. You can choose to either focus on what's wrong or what's right, what's good or what's bad, what you've done wrong, or what you're learning to do differently. The choice is yours. When life pushes you down, fall forward.

Change Your Mental Scenery

Much of how we feel about life comes from the way we look at it. I've always loved this little poem:

> Two men look out the same prison bars.
> One sees mud, and the other stars.
>
> —FREDERICK LANGBRIDGE

Both men were in prison, mud and stars were equally present, but I think the man who focused on the stars felt happier than the man who only saw mud. You may feel like your life is a prison and that you have a life sentence. There is no leaving your circumstances, but how you live in them and look at them will impact your levels of well-being, not only emotionally, but mentally, spiritually, relationally, and physically.

Those of us who are more naturally pessimistic may become somewhat skeptical when we're challenged to think more positively. We think we're being realistic, and we don't want to fool ourselves into looking at something more positively than it warrants. Lee Ross, professor and graduate advisor at Stanford University, says that optimism "is not about providing a recipe for self-deception. The world can be a horrible, cruel place, and at the same time it can be wonderful and abundant. These are both truths. There is not a halfway point; there is only choosing which truth to put in your personal foreground."[4]

• • • • • • • • • • **A Good Death** • • • • • • • • •

Randy Pausch was an inspiration to millions of people and an extraordinary example of looking at the stars from prison bars. Diagnosed with terminal pancreatic cancer in the fall of 2007, he wanted to leave his young children some final thoughts about living life well. He did this in his last lecture for his students at Carnegie-Mellon University, and it became a YouTube sensation and turned into a bestselling book called *The Last Lecture.* Living each day to the fullest, extracting every drop of what each day held was in Randy's foreground, dying of cancer stayed in the background and he kept it in the background as long as he could.

It's not that he lived in denial. He was very honest with his diagnosis and prognosis. As anyone would be tempted to do, he could have fallen into self-pity, asking the question *Why me?* He could have worried, *How will my family function without me?* He could have spent his remaining time focusing on the mud and prison bars, but he did neither. He lived each day loving, learning, laughing, and teaching others how to turn lemons into lemonade. He died in July 2008.

• •

The apostle Paul was no stranger to suffering. He was shipwrecked, unfairly imprisoned, mocked, humiliated, and beaten and left for dead. He could have let his mind dwell on the mud in his prison cell. Instead he gives us this advice about what to put in the foreground of our minds. He writes, "Whatever is true, whatever is noble, whatever is right, whatever is pure, whatever is lovely, whatever is admirable— if anything is excellent or praiseworthy—think about such things" (Philippians 4:8).

I just returned from a trip to Budapest, Hungary. While there, I toured the Jewish synagogue and learned some incredible stories about courageous men and women who, while living in hell, created bits of heaven by helping others during the Holocaust. They demonstrated that it's possible, even under the worst of circumstances, not only to endure, but to find purpose, meaning, and even pockets of joy as they lived their lives loving, helping, and serving others.

Suffering

There are two types of suffering, necessary suffering and unnecessary suffering.[5] Necessary suffering is important. It helps us grieve our losses and deal with our pain. It is used by God to teach us what's important and to help us grow up and let go of foolish things. Necessary suffering helps us find God and our true selves instead of losing our way through life with temporal delights and deceptive thinking. Necessary suffering is part of living in a sinful and broken world. Things are not as they should be.

Unnecessary suffering is our poor response to necessary suffering. It rises out of our unrealistic expectations, the lies we believe, our bad habits, and our negative emotions such as self-pity, envy, greed, jealousy, resentment, pride, and shame.

Stacy was laid off from a job she loved. It came as a total surprise. The company gave some vague reason, but Stacy couldn't wrap her arms around why they let her go. She was a good employee and she always received positive reviews. She felt hurt and angry as anyone would. That's the first part of the story and the beginning of necessary suffering. Now it was Stacy's turn to add her part of the story. What would she do with the reality of her layoff?

One ending could have been that Stacy looked for the diamonds in the situation. For example, she now had the opportunity to stay home with her three children during the summer months and still collect unemployment benefits. She had always felt guilty putting them in day care over the summer months, and now she could be home with them and still bring in some income. In addition, she could have trusted that God had reasons unknown to her why he moved her out of that environment and that he would use this situation for her good.

Although Stacy mentally acknowledged those benefits, she chose to focus on the mud, and by doing so, added unnecessary suffering to her plate. She obsessed with why she had been let go. Day and night she would try to figure what went wrong and all she could talk about was her pain. Stacy felt self-conscious and thought other people must know she had been laid off and that they would be talking about her. Soon she didn't want to leave her home.

Stacy felt real pain when her employer let her go. Perhaps he wanted to hire a relative or he was experiencing financial shortages and was too proud to tell her. She didn't know why, but she added extra suffering through her negative self-talk, self-consciousness, and overanalyzing the situation.

The writer of Hebrews counsels us in this area. He writes,

> Since we are surrounded by such a huge crowd of witnesses to the life of faith, let us strip off *every weight that slows us down,* especially the sin that so easily trips us up. And let us run with endurance the race God has set before us. We do this by keeping our eyes on Jesus, the champion who initiates and perfects our faith. Because of the joy awaiting him, he endured the cross, disregarding its shame. Now he

is seated in the place of honor beside God's throne (Hebrews 12:1-3 NLT).

Unnecessary suffering results from our inability to see things with new eyes and make lemonade from lemons. The verses above tell us to strip off every weight that slows us down including our negative emotions and wrong thinking. Instead we are to learn to put Jesus in the foreground, not our difficult situation.

Jesus said, "I have told you these things, so that in me you may have peace. In this world you *will* have trouble. But take heart! I have overcome the world" (John 16:33). You are not alone. Jesus knows the pain of living in a broken down world. He is present to help you, to guide you, and to comfort you. Your suffering is not meaningless and God will redeem it if you let him.

The recipe for luscious lemonade is two parts faith, one part attitude, and one part skill. New attitudes and skills we can learn, train, and practice so that we do them better, but we must be willing. Do it and the benefits will bless your heart and others with peace and joy even in the midst of pain.

Questions for
Thought and Discussion

1. Respond to the author's statement, "Happiness is not about feeling fabulous and never feeling pain. It's about feeling pain and finding purpose." Do you agree or disagree? How have you done that in past situations?

2. Rick Warren says in *The Purpose-Driven Life,*

> If you really desire to be used by God, you *must* understand
> this powerful truth: The very experiences that you have
> resented or regretted most in life—the ones you've wanted
> to hide and forget—are the experiences God wants to use
> to help others. They are your ministry![6]

How can you cooperate with God by writing a positive ending to
your difficult situation?

3. The author states that "adversity not only reveals our character,
it shapes it." Read Romans 5:3-4. What character qualities and
strengths have you developed through the very hardships you've
endured?

4. How do those who do not profess Christ as Savior and Lord still
make lemonade when adversity strikes? What is lacking in a person
who knows Christ yet stays stuck sucking on lemons instead of
making lemonade?

5. Read Psalm 39:1-7. The psalmist struggles with his negative emotions and how he is going to handle them. What gives him perspective? How can you put what you're dealing with in the background and create a story around it that makes God famous?

6. Discuss and review the skills you have learned throughout this book that will help you be more capable of transforming adversity.

CHAPTER 11

Giving Thanks Is Not Just for Thanksgiving

Gratitude takes nothing for granted, is never unresponsive, is constantly awakening to new wonder, and to praise of the goodness of God.

THOMAS MERTON

Be joyful always; pray continually; give thanks in all circumstances, for this is God's will for you in Christ Jesus.

PAUL, IN 1 THESSALONIANS 5:16-18

Thank you, Lord Jesus, for what you have given me, for what you have taken away from me, and for what you have left me.

THOMAS MORE

THANKSGIVING IS TRADITIONALLY A DAY FOR FOOD, family gatherings, football, and giving thanks. When everyone is gathered at our table, before we pray, my husband, Howard, always asks us to share what we're thankful for. I'm sure many of you do likewise. If you want to be happier, from now on, don't make thanksgiving a once a year occasion. I don't mean cook a large turkey dinner every so often, but practice gratitude frequently.

Thanksgiving Is a Command

Biblically speaking, gratitude is not an option. God commands it and as believers, it is to permeate our lives (Colossians 3:15-17). However, early on in my Christian life I found it difficult to give thanks in all circumstances. As a counselor, at times I thought it bordered on craziness. I would ask myself how it was possible to be thankful for losing a job or a loved one. How could a person be thankful for a rotten childhood? Yet as I have grown in my journey of experiencing more happiness, gratitude is an important positive emotion we must cultivate.

This spring I was speaking at a retreat, and a woman shared with me that her only son was killed in a motorcycle accident. I was not talking on the topic of grief or gratitude, but spontaneously she added, "I can't give thanks *for* all things but I can give thanks *in* all things."

What an important distinction. She went on to say, "I'm thankful that I had my son for 24 years. I'm thankful he didn't suffer when he died. I'm thankful for so many wonderful friends. And I'm thankful that he died doing what he loved." Her attitude made all the difference in how she processed her grief. Gratitude didn't take away her pain, but it transformed it into praise instead of bitterness.

On the other hand, Shirley and her husband lost a lot of money in an unjust lawsuit. Relatives took sides and the family split apart. Overwhelmed with anger and hurt, Shirley began to slip into the pit of despair. "I see no purpose in living anymore," she cried. "I can't believe God is letting this happen to me. I will never forgive them for what they have done."

If there is no repentance, Shirley may never be able to reconcile with her relatives, but if she wants to be happier, she will have to learn how to let go of her negative thoughts and toxic emotions and someday forgive them. Shirley can't wait until her circumstances change or her relatives repent in order to feel happier, or it may never happen. She has no control over those things. What Shirley can do is learn to be thankful *in* all circumstances and to look for the silver lining in what she is experiencing.

Life happens. Good things and bad things come to everyone. But those who learn to be thankful in all things can maintain their mental and emotional well-being even in the midst of hardship because they trust in a good God who is in control of all of life.

The Benefits of Gratitude

The psalmist unapologetically proclaims, "It is good to give thanks to the LORD" (Psalm 92:2 NLT). Practicing thanksgiving protects us from slipping into grumbling and complaining when life does not go our way or we do not get what we want. We often see life through the lens of entitlement instead of gratitude. We think God (or people, or the universe) owes us something and when we don't get what we think we deserve, we are miserable and believe we have every right to feel that way.

Being thankful in all things helps us fight off those feelings of entitlement, resentment, and bitterness that want to wrap themselves around our spirit. Psychologist Sonja Lyubomirsky says that "gratitude is an antidote to negative emotions, a neutralizer of envy, avarice, hostility, worry, and irritation."[1]

Dr. Lyubomirsky reports study after study on the effects of gratitude. She says when people are thankful, they are more optimistic about life, physically healthier, less stressed, more resilient, more willing to help others, and less likely to suffer from depression and anxiety.[2] Research also indicates that

> victims of profound tragedies (e.g., the September 11 terrorist attacks) who experience gratitude and positive emotions tend to be the ones who recover. People suffering from disasters, deadly diseases, or human loss appear to cope better as a result of being able to see some benefit in their predicaments.[3]

Gratitude Helps Us See Our Situation Differently

In an excerpt from his new book *Always Looking Up: So Much to Be Grateful For,* actor Michael J. Fox said,

> For everything this disease has taken, something with greater value has been given—sometimes just a marker that points me in a new direction that I might not otherwise have traveled. So, sure, it may be one step forward and two steps back, but after a time with Parkinson's, I've learned that what is important is making that one step count; always looking up.[4]

Gratitude keeps Michael J. Fox's mind from dwelling on what he's lost through Parkinson's disease, moving his thoughts to appreciating what he has gained. It also empowers him to contain and release whatever unhappy feelings he experiences so that he is able to feel happy with his life, as well as find purpose and meaning in his illness.

• • • • • • • • • • **The Lens of Gratitude** • • • • • • • • •

Amy was leaving her house for an important business meeting when she noticed her car had a flat tire. Immediately she began to grumble and complain, frustrated with her bad luck. While on hold with AAA to come and change her tire, she stewed and fumed until she stopped and began to look at the situation through the lens of gratitude. Amy told herself that she was thankful that she was not driving on the highway when her tire went flat. She felt grateful that she was still at home and that she did not have to stand in the cold nor was she in any danger while she waited for AAA to come and help her.

Choosing gratitude didn't get Amy to her meeting on time, but it certainly got her to work in a much better frame of mind than had she stayed focused on her flat tire.

• •

Gratitude Helps Us Embrace God's Goodness and Feel Happier

In addition to the benefits of a changed perspective and a calmer spirit, practicing gratitude reminds us that everything that happens to us is a gift—even the things we never asked for or didn't want. Thomas Merton says,

> To be grateful is to recognize the love of God in everything He has given us—and He has given us everything. Every breath we draw is a gift of His love, every moment of existence is a grace, for it brings with it immense graces from Him. Gratitude therefore takes nothing for granted, is never unresponsive, is constantly awakening to new wonder and to praise of the goodness of God. For the grateful person knows that God is good, not by hearsay but by experience. And that is what makes all the difference.[5]

My good friend Georgia Shaffer chronicles her brush with death through a bone-marrow transplant for breast cancer in her book *A Gift of Mourning Glories*. Although she would never have chosen it, she describes her cancer and subsequent transplant as an unwanted gift that not only taught her significant life lessons but allowed her to experience God's love and goodness to her in ways she would not have otherwise known.[6]

Psychologist Lewis Smedes, after surviving a serious illness, wrote,

> It was then I learned that gratitude is the best feeling I would ever have, the ultimate joy of living. It was better than sex, better than winning a lottery, better than watching your daughter graduate from college, better and deeper than any other feeling; it is perhaps, the genesis of all other really good feelings in the human repertoire. I am sure that nothing in life can ever match the feeling of being held in being by the gracious energy percolating from the abyss where beats the loving heart of God.[7]

The psalmist declares, "Give thanks to the LORD, for he is good; his love endures forever" (Psalm 107:1).

Gratitude Helps Us Develop Humility

Regularly giving thanks to God puts us into our rightful place as dependent human beings and cultivates an inner posture of humility. Gratitude reminds us that we are not owed anything. As creatures we are dependent upon God for everything.[8] Jesus, although he was God in human form, depended on and gave thanks to God, his Father (see Matthew 14:19; 15:36; 26:26 for examples).

Shirley's family turmoil as well as financial loss is no doubt extremely painful for her, but in the midst of it, God might be trying to teach her how to trust him more, and her money less. Perhaps Shirley's real need isn't for more justice or fairness, but rather to deepen her faith by trusting God, forgiving those who sinned against her, and learning how to overcome evil with good. Gratitude might seem like the last thing on Shirley's mind, but it will be one of the most important things she can choose to move beyond her anger and her pain.

Gratitude develops and strengthens our ability to humbly trust God to know best what we need most.

Gratitude Helps Us Look at People Differently

If you're having relationship difficulties, try looking for specific things about that person that you can be thankful for instead of focusing on their negative qualities. We've already talked about the thought–feeling connection. When you look for someone's good qualities and are thankful for them, it will help you feel closer and more connected as well as have more positive emotions. The apostle Paul regularly gave thanks for the people God put into his life. How would the atmosphere in your family change if people sincerely expressed their appreciation as well as gratitude for one another?

Marie had just returned from a women's retreat all excited about what the Lord had taught her. When she walked in the door she was greeted by three filthy children and a house full of fast-food wrappers, dirty dishes, and unopened mail. Immediately she felt her joy replaced with irritation. She thought to herself, *Why do I have to come home to this mess?*

Alert to what was happening in her mood, Marie chose to change her mental channel from grumbling to gratitude. She looked at the situation again and this time she saw her children grinning from ear to ear, happy that they had a great time with their dad over the weekend. Together they had built a new swingset in the yard, and her husband was still outside finishing it up. Marie felt grateful for her children and for her husband, who had spent his entire weekend playing with them and building an outdoor play set. It was a small thing that he didn't bathe the kids or clean everything up before she got home. She chose not to let it rob her of her joy.

Later on that evening, Marie and her husband washed up the kids, straightened up the mess, and enjoyed their evening together talking about what she had learned at the retreat. Had she given in to her initial negative feelings and started criticizing and complaining when she first got home, their evening would have turned out very differently.

Practicing Gratitude

Many of us see being thankful as an exercise in counting our blessings, and indeed that is one form of practicing gratitude, but it isn't enough. In the same way that our physical workout needs to be varied if we want maximum results, we need to learn additional ways to incorporate gratitude into our lives in order to reap the maximum rewards. Therefore, mix it up so that your aptitude for gratitude stays high.

Pay Attention

I've encouraged you to pay attention, wake up, and be mindful throughout this book, but it's so important to our well-being that it bears repeating. It's hard to be thankful for something you don't notice. Just as Marie had to mentally switch channels in order to move beyond what she first saw when she walked into her messy house, we need to open our physical eyes and the eyes of our heart, to God's goodness, beauty, and provisions all around us. Don Postema writes,

> How much more breathtaking our lives could be if we were deeply aware of the gifts of God that surround us and engage us. If we were awake![9]

I haven't spent much time outdoors because I've been traveling and writing. But when I walked my dog yesterday, I became aware that my garden was overgrown with weeds. Later on, one of my clients complimented me on all my beautiful flowers. I hadn't noticed them because all I saw were the weeds. When I told her that, she said, "I didn't see any weeds at all, I only noticed flowers." We laughed. They were both there. My garden has beautiful flowers *and* a lot of weeds. It reminded me of life—that what we focus on impacts our well-being and our levels of happiness.

Don't get me wrong, there is time to pay attention to the weeds. Ignoring them would eventually ruin my garden and it feels good to pull them and clean up my yard. But I will never have a garden with no weeds, and we will never have a life with no stress or hassles. That is saved for heaven. So be intentional and look for things to be thankful for, especially if you find your day filled with weeds.

Learn to Savor the Moment

I'd like you to try something that I do in my seminars. Take a chocolate-covered raisin and hold it in your hand. Notice everything you can about it. For example, it has a shiny chocolate coating, deep ridges, and if you hold it long enough you will notice the chocolate begins to melt in your palm. Before that happens, pop it into your mouth, but don't chew it or swallow it. Just let it be and focus all your attention on that little morsel. Let your tongue caress the smooth chocolate and then the ridges of the raisin. Notice the different flavors and textures. What do you smell? See how long you can make it last.

How do you feel in this moment? Did you enjoy that tiny little chocolate raisin in a different way than you would have if you had mindlessly grabbed and eaten an entire handful? (If you don't like chocolate or raisins, use something else like a jelly bean or a caramel.) Can you feel grateful for the simple pleasure of a moment of sweetness?

This exercise helps you learn not only how to pay attention, but how to recognize the miraculous in mundane moments. Happiness often comes in moments, and if we don't notice or take the time to savor, we miss them. One of my favorite savoring moments is watching hummingbirds at my feeder. I feel blessed when they choose my house to nourish themselves. Being aware of opportunities God gives us to enjoy his creation, people, and himself are all important aspects of learning how to be happy.

The Lord says, "Be still, and know that I am God" (Psalm 46:10). You may have eaten many Raisinets in the past, but never slowed the process enough to savor them. In a similar way, we rush through our time with God and don't pause to experience his still small voice, or the pleasure of his presence. The psalmist says that there isn't any better feeling than experiencing God's presence (Psalm 16:11). Heaven is the fullness of that experience. Hell is the absence of it. On earth we have tastes of heaven and tastes of hell. Sadly, we are often too busy to be still enough long enough to savor God or what he gives us. Instead we are focused on doing more, but we enjoy it less. No wonder we struggle even as Christians to actually feel his peace, his joy, his love, and his hope.

Some people feel guilty enjoying God-given pleasures because they believe God alone is all we need for happiness. This is wrong thinking. Of course our primary source of joy is in loving God and being in his presence, but that doesn't exclude enjoying the things he has made and what he has given us to enjoy. God takes pleasure in our pleasure, as long as it is not taking his place. Be grateful for it.

Help Someone Less Fortunate Than You Are

Nothing helps us faster to be grateful for what we have than spending some time with someone who has less. I don't believe comparing one's self with others is usually a good practice because most of the time we compare up and as a result we want more and are not grateful.

We see our neighbors with the new tractor or fancy granite countertops and all of a sudden our mower or kitchen is outdated and not good enough. We look at magazine covers of actresses our age who look years younger and we feel old, fat, and ugly, and think Botox and liposuction will make us happy.

If you're struggling with the have nots, spend some time volunteering in a homeless shelter, soup kitchen, hospital oncology ward, or nursing home and you will come back from these encounters more grateful for your health, your family, your home, and a simple meal. It will help you remember that life and happiness is not about getting more but enjoying and appreciating what you have.

Tell Someone "Thank You"

The Bible tells a story of ten lepers who were all healed of their leprosy but only one of them returned to say "Thank you." He ran back to Jesus, praising God for his incredible goodness to him. Jesus asked him, "What happened to the other nine that were also healed?" (see Luke 17:11-19).

Sometimes we're aware that we've been treated kindly or blessed by someone but we just don't personally express our appreciation. Even writing simple thank you letters for Christmas or birthday gifts is neglected by many individuals. Expressing your gratitude not only encourages the giver, it blesses us. Psychologist and clinical researcher Christopher Peterson experimented with the benefits of expressing gratitude. Here was what he told people:

> Think of all the people—parents, friends, teachers, coaches, teammates, employers, and so on—who have been especially kind to you but have never heard you express your gratitude. This exercise tells us to write a gratitude letter to one of these

individuals, describing in concrete terms why you are grateful. If possible, deliver it personally and have the person read the letter in your presence. If this is not possible, then mail or fax the letter and follow it up with a phone call.[10]

The results were indisputable. Peterson said, "They 'work' 100 percent of the time in the sense that the recipient is moved, often to tears, and the sender is gratified as well. Studies have also shown that 'the habitually grateful among us are happier than those who are not.'"[11]

Count Your Blessings in Different Ways

When I ask my clients to think about what's good in their lives, they often give thanks for their health, their children, their job, and so on. Studies show that counting your blessings at the end of your day, rather than in the morning, yields better benefits. When we go to sleep feeling positive, it's more likely we will wake up positive.[12]

To vary this practice so that it doesn't become trite or routine, think about three good things that happened during the day (whether big or small) and write down why you believe they happened.[13] For example, I might recall the hummingbird at my feeder, my publisher liked my manuscript, and that my husband took me out for a nice dinner.

Contemplating why these things may have happened helps me dig deeper and be more aware. For example, I feel thankful that my publisher liked my manuscript, but asking myself why my publisher liked my book might help me remember and feel grateful that God enabled me to write it, and that he has given me gifts to use for his glory. Thinking more about why my husband took me out for a nice dinner helps me feel loved instead of just satiated…or thankful that I didn't have to cook dinner myself.

Be Grateful for Being You

Self-acceptance is a wonderful gift you can give yourself. Many of us are extremely self-critical, magnifying our flaws and minimizing our God-given talents, abilities, and strengths we've developed as a benefit of discipline or difficulties we've endured. As a result, we feel chronically unhappy with ourselves and disappointed that we aren't better than we are. Worse than that, we wish that we were someone other than who we are.

God's Word tells us that God designed us from scratch. There isn't another human being made quite like you (Psalm 139). We will never be transformed into a different person, but we can, with God's help, become the best version of ourselves, which is the person he created us to be. It is not prideful to have a good self-image or positive self-esteem. The kind of pride that God abhors is when you think you don't need him or that you know better than he does how to run your life.

Start today to give thanks for who God made you to be. Be appreciative of your unique talents, abilities, gifts, and strengths. One of my clients once told me, "I'm not yet who I want to be, but I'm not still who I used to be, and for that I'm grateful."

Praise and Worship

The apostle Paul said that thanklessness is one of the consequences of our sinful nature. He writes, "Although they knew God, they neither glorified him as God nor gave *thanks* to him, but their thinking became futile and their foolish hearts were darkened" (Romans 1:21). Paul teaches that God has made himself knowable through what he has created so humankind is without an excuse. Our problem isn't that we can't see him; it's that we fail to glorify him and give him thanks. Instead of worshipping God, we worship the things he's created (see Romans 1:18-32).

Intentionally and gratefully acknowledging God's holiness, his goodness, and his greatness through praise and worship keeps us mindful that we are wonderful but broken creatures and need him for everything. It also reminds us that created things are temporary, but God's kingdom remains. The writer of Hebrews says, "Since we are receiving a kingdom that cannot be shaken, let us be thankful, and so worship

God acceptably with reverence and awe, for our God is a consuming fire" (Hebrews 12:28-29; see also Psalms 95, 100, and 136). Grateful praise reminds us that loving God is primary and the love of his creation secondary.

Sacrifice of Thanksgiving

Lauren's husband, Jerry, just got laid off from his job. Distraught, she asked me why God would allow so many hard things in her life. Five years ago she had been diagnosed with ovarian cancer. Then she lost her job. Debts from the last layoff and past medical expenses were just about paid, and they were starting to save a little for their children's future. Now this.

"I can't take any more," Lauren cried. "Why is God allowing this to happen to me?" Sometimes we don't know why, but we can still choose to thank God for who he is, even if we don't understand him.

Like Lauren, King David went through a period of depression, confusion, and despair. He said, "I am in pain and distress; may your salvation, O God, protect me. I will praise God's name in song and glorify him with thanksgiving. This will please the LORD more than an ox, more than a bull with its horns and hoofs" (Psalm 69:29-30).

When you are scared, angry, lonely, and depressed, when you don't *feel* thankful, give thanks anyway as an act of obedience. Henri Nouwen writes,

> Gratitude as a discipline involves a conscious choice. I can choose to be grateful even when my emotions and feelings are still steeped in hurt and resentment. It is amazing how many occasions present themselves in which I can choose gratitude instead of a complaint. I can choose to be grateful when I am criticized, even when my heart still responds in bitterness. I can choose to speak about goodness and beauty, even when my inner eye still looks for someone to accuse or something to call ugly.[14]

When you're depressed with no appetite, you must choose to eat something in order to give the food a chance to nourish your body. Praise and thank God even when you have no appetite to do so, and allow the sacrifice of praise and thanksgiving to nourish your soul.

Questions for
Thought and Discussion

1. Do you agree that having gratitude is something we need to learn and choose to do versus spontaneously feel? Why or why not?

2. Reflect on the author's comment, "Gratitude reminds us of our place as creatures." Do you agree or disagree? How does practicing gratitude build humility?

3. Read the story in Luke 7:36-50 and reflect upon the different responses of these two characters. What made one more grateful than the other? Which person do you most identify with?

4. Read Exodus 16. How have you been like the Israelites? Notice how you feel after you grumble and complain versus how you feel after you've intentionally expressed thanks.

5. Write a letter of gratitude to someone as suggested on page 220. How did you feel while writing it? How did the recipient feel? Did it make you happy to see him or her happy?

6. What steps can you take to become more appreciative of the small joys in your daily life? How can you practice savoring life, like you did in the Raisinet exercise?

7. Imagine that your entire life you've longed to be a rose. You've admired their beauty and fragrance, but no matter how hard you've worked at it, it hasn't happened. And now you're frustrated and unhappy. (This is like trying to live out the script, *I should be more than I am.*)

I'd like you to try something different. Instead of focusing on what you are not, I'd like you to pay attention to what kind of flower God has made you to be. Is it a daffodil? A bleeding heart?

A coneflower? A daisy? You will need to accept that God didn't make you a rose. But do understand this—you were made to be beautiful.

Can you begin to be thankful for who God made you to be? Instead of striving to become someone you are not, how can you work with God's help to become the most vibrant, fragrant, healthy person you can be?

A Few Final Thoughts

OVER THE YEARS, I HAVE READ HUNDREDS OF personal-growth type books, both Christian and secular. I've learned a great deal, but I've noticed that if I don't practice what I've learned, nothing really changes.

If you're anything like me, you've read through this book rather quickly so you could know how to become a happier person. And I trust that you've been encouraged that there are some real things you can do to change. However, I know from personal experience that reading something in a book rarely translates into life-changing action without some additional steps.

Recently one of my clients told me she joined a group that meets weekly so they can train to run a 5K race. She's never run in a race before and has always wanted to. Each week the group meets to learn the next steps for a successful finish and then they actually do it. They run together.

That is a beautiful picture of the body of Christ. James tell us, "Do not merely listen to the word, and so deceive yourselves. Do what it says" (James 1:22). I encourage you to gather together some others who, like you, want to learn how to be holier and happier people. Study this book together. Do the exercises, read the scriptures, help one another get out of the pit, challenge each other to grow and become more beautiful, encourage one another in your training regimens, pray for one another, be thankful for one another and, above all, love each other through your successes and failures.

My prayer for you is that you now understand it's not enough to just *want* to be happy. You must practice the skills that will get you there. Practicing them and staying focused is much easier and more fun when you're with a group of like-minded people. With God's help, I know you can do it. He wants you to be holy and happy, and so do I.

Notes

Introduction

1. John Piper, www.desiringgod.org/ResourceLibrary/Articles/ByDate/2006/1797_We_ Want_You.
2. Blaise Pascal, as quoted in James M. Houston, *Mind on Fire: A Faith for the Skeptical and Indifferent* (Minneapolis: Bethany, 1997), 108.
3. Sheldon Vanauken, *A Severe Mercy* (New York: Harper & Row, 1977), 190.

Chapter 1—Stories and Scripts

1. Gary A. Haugen, *Just Courage: God's Great Expedition for the Restless Christian* (Downers Grove, IL: InterVarsity Press, 2009), 16-17.
2. Sonja Lyubomirsky, *The How of Happiness* (New York: Penguin, 2007), 48.
3. Jonathan Haidt, *The Happiness Hypothesis: Finding Modern Truth in Ancient Wisdom* (New York: Basic Books, 2006), 82. I first heard this phrase used in this book.
4. C.S. Lewis, *The Problem of Pain* (New York: Macmillan, 1962), 93.
5. Arthur Schopenhauer, *The World as Will and Representation*, tr. E.F.J. Payne (New York: Dover, 1966), 309.

Chapter 2—Elephants Out of Control

1. Jonathan Haidt, *The Happiness Hypothesis: Finding Modern Truth in Ancient Wisdom* (New York, NY: Basic Books, 2006). Haidt uses the metaphor of an elephant and its rider throughout his book to describe the war between our consciously controlled thoughts (the rider) and our biological impulses, intuitions, emotions, desires—in essence, everything else (the elephant). Since I had personal experience with an elephant and its helpless owner, I found it a very compelling analogy.
2. Dallas Willard, *Renovation of the Heart* (Colorado Springs, CO: NavPress, 2002), 124.
3. Thomas à Kempis, *Of The Imitation of Christ* (Springdale, PA: Whitaker House, 1981), 95.
4. Thornton Wilder, *Our Town* (New York: HarperCollins, 2003), 100.
5. http://www.barna.org/barna-update/article/16-teensnext-gen/25-young-adults-and-liberals-st...

Chapter 3—Stuck in the Pit

1. Harvard Mental Health Letter (Boston: 2006), 8.

2. Sonja Lyubomirsky, *The How of Happiness* (New York: Penguin, 2007), 113.

3. Lyubomirsky, 244-245.

4. John Calvin, as quoted by Don Postema, *Space for God* (Grand Rapids, MI: CRC Publications, 1997), 82.

5. Lyubomirsky, 241.

6. Jonathan Haidt, *The Happiness Hypothesis: Finding Modern Truth in Ancient Wisdom* (New York: Basic Books, 2006), 78.

7. Lyubomirsky, 251.

8. Malcolm Gladwell, *Blink* (New York: Hachette Book Group USA, 2005), 206.

9. Charles Spurgeon, *Joy in Your Life* (New Kensington, PA: Whitaker House, 1998), 125.

Chapter 4—Recalculating

1. Jonathan Haidt, *The Happiness Hypothesis: Finding Modern Truth in Ancient Wisdom* (New York: Basic Books, 2006), 26.

2. Daniel Goleman, *Social Intelligence* (New York: Bantam Dell, 2006), 152.

3. Portia Nelson, "Autobiography in Five Short Chapters," from *There's a Hole in My Sidewalk* (Hillsboro, OR: Beyond Words Publishing, 1993). Copyright © 1993 by Portia Nelson, from the book *There's a Hole in My Sidewalk.* Reprinted with permission from Beyond Words Publishing, Hillsboro, Oregon.

4. For more information on how to invite your partner to make healthy changes, see my book *The Emotionally Destructive Relationship* (Eugene, OR: Harvest House Publishers, 2007).

5. Thomas Merton, *Thoughts in Solitude* (New York: Farrar, Straus and Giroux, 1958), 4.

6. Oswald Chambers, *Devotions for a Deeper Life,* ed. Glenn D. Black (Grand Rapids, MI: Zondervan Publishing House, 1995), 163.

Chapter 5—A New Way of Seeing

1. *W Magazine,* April 2009, 48.

2. A.W. Tozer, *The Pursuit of God* (Camp Hill, PA: Christian Publications, 1993), 10.

3. David G. Myers, *The American Paradox* (New Haven, CT: Yale University Press, 2000), xi.

4. *NIV Introduction to the Book of Job* (Grand Rapids, MI: Zondervan Publishing House, 1995), 723.

5. For more on the story and what God might be up to during these particularly difficult times, see my book *How to Live Right When Your Life Goes Wrong* (Colorado Springs, CO: WaterBrook Press, 2003), chapter 1.

6. Wayne Grudem, *Systematic Theology* (Leicester, Great Britain: Inter-Varsity Press, and Grand Rapids, MI: Zondervan Publishing House, 1994), 197.

7. Tozer, *Knowledge of the Holy* (San Francisco: HarperOne, 1992),82.

8. John Eldredge, "Major and Minor Themes," in Kelly Monroe Kullberg and Lael Arrington, *A Faith and Culture Devotional* (Grand Rapids, MI: Zondervan, 2008), 151.

9. Kullberg and Arrington, 152.

10. Kullberg and Arrington, 153.

11. Richard Rohr, *Collected Talks*, vol. 2 (Cincinnati: St. Anthony Messenger, 2005), CD presentation.

12. Kullberg and Arrington, 277.

13. Kenneth W. Osbeck, *101 Hymn Stories* (Grand Rapids, MI: Kregel, 1982), 58.

Chapter 6—Fall in Love

1. François Fenelon, *Christian Perfection* (New York: Harper & Row, 1975), 13.

2. Oswald Chambers, *My Utmost for His Highest* (July 30), 154.

3. David Naugle, *Reordered Love, Reordered Lives: Learning the Deep Meaning of Happiness* (Grand Rapids, MI: William B. Eerdmans Publishing, 2008), 22.

4. Naugle, 47.

5. Henri J.M. Nouwen, *The Genesee Diary* (New York: Doubleday 1976), 76-77.

6. James Houston, *In Pursuit of Happiness: Finding Genuine Fulfillment in Life* (Colorado Springs, CO: NavPress, 1996), 254.

7. Father Pedro Arrupe, The General Society of Jesus.

8. George Macdonald, *Discovering the Character of God* (Minneapolis: Bethany House, 1989), 21.

9. John Piper, *When I Don't Desire God* (Wheaton, IL: Good News Publishers, 2004), 33.

10. Mike Mason, *Champagne for the Soul* (Colorado Springs, CO: WaterBrook), 14.

Chapter 7—A Beautiful You

1. www.worldwildlife.org/species/finder/monarchbutterflies/monarchbutterflies.html.

2. Thomas Dubay, *The Evidential Power of Beauty* (San Francisco: Ignatius Press, 1999), 56.

3. Dallas Willard, *Renovation of the Heart* (Colorado Springs, CO: NavPress, 2002), 54.

4. A.W. Tozer, *The Best of A.W. Tozer* (Grand Rapids, MI: Baker Books, 1978), 112.

5. C.S. Lewis, *Mere Christianity* (New York: MacMillan Publishers, 1973), 86.

6. Jonathan Haidt, *The Happiness Hypothesis: Finding Modern Truth in Ancient Wisdom* (New York: Basic Books, 2006), 157.

7. Haidt, 157, emphasis added.

8. John Piper, *When I Don't Desire God* (Wheaton, IL: Good News Publishers, 2004), 33.

Chapter 8—Training Elephants and Human Hearts

1. Thomas à Kempis, *Of the Imitation of Christ* (Springdale, PA: Whitaker House, 1981), 58.

2. Abraham Joshua Heschel, *Man Is Not Alone* (New York: Farrar, Straus and Giroux, 1951), 186, 189.

3. Dallas Willard, *The Spirit of the Disciplines* (New York: Harper Collins Publishers, 1988), 167.

4. Blaise Pascal, as quoted by Douglas V. Steer, *Prayer in the Contemporary World* (New York: Department of Publication Services, 1966), 4.

5. Ruth Haley Barton, *Beyond Words; An Invitation to Solitude and Silence* (Atlanta: Conversations Journal, vol. 5:2), 10.

6. Arthur Bennett, ed., *The Valley of Vision: A Collection of Puritan Prayers and Devotions* (Carlisle, PA: Banner of Truth, 1975), 13. Used with permission.

7. M. Scott Peck, *The Road Less Traveled*, (New York: Simon & Schuster, 1978), 271.

8. François Fenelon, *Christian Perfection*, (New York: Harper & Row, 1975) 3.

9. Ed Welch, "Unchained," publication of True life Ministry, Fall 2005, 8.

10. Leonard Sweet, *Out of the Question...Into the Mystery: Getting Lost in the Godlife Relationship* (Colorado Springs, CO: WaterBrook 2004), 126.

Chapter 9—The Intentional Life

1. Sonja Lyubomirsky, *The How of Happiness* (New York: Penguin, 2007), 68.

2. See Dr. Archibald Hart's book *Thrilled to Death* (Nashville: Thomas Nelson, 2007).

3. Thomas Kelly, *A Testament of Devotion* (New York: Harper & Brothers, 1941), 109.

4. www.awakengggennneratttion.com/thoughts/befuled/187. Dr. Collins has written a book called *The Language of God* (New York: Free Press, 2006).

5. For more information on dealing with painful relationship issues, see my books *The Emotionally Destructive Relationship* (Eugene, OR: Harvest House Publishers, 2007) and *How to Act Right When Your Spouse Acts Wrong* (Colorado Springs, CO: WaterBrook Press, 2001).

6. Lyubomirsky, chapters 5 and 6; Jonathan Haidt, *The Happiness Hypothesis: Finding Modern Truth in Ancient Wisdom* (New York: Basic Books, 2006), chapters 6 and 7

7. In a study cited in *A Primer in Positive Psychology* (34-35), college students were asked which satisfied them more—having a good time or helping others. To answer that question, they were told to pursue one pleasurable activity (of their own choice) and one philanthropic activity (of their own choice), then write a brief paper about their reactions to each. Overwhelmingly, the students discovered that fun was pleasurable for the moment, but deeper satisfaction came when they helped others or did something good for someone else.

8. Tal Ben-Shahar, *Happier* (New York: McGraw-Hill, 2007), 86.

9. Jan Johnson, *Enjoying the Presence of God* (Colorado Springs, CO: NavPress, 1996), 70.

10. www.quotationspage.com/quote/George_Bernard_Shaw/61.

Chapter 10—Making Lemonade

1. www.alexslemonade.org

2. Sonja Lyubomirsky, *The How of Happiness* (New York: Penguin, 2007), chapter 6 "Managing Stress, Hardship, and Trauma."

3. James W. Pennebaker, *Opening Up: The Healing Power of Expressing Emotions,* rev. ed. (New York: Guilford, 1997).

4. Lee Ross, as quoted by Lyubomirsky, 111.

5. Rami Shapiro, *The Way of Solomon* (New York: HarperOne, 2000), 106.

6. Rick Warren, *The Purpose Driven Life* (Grand Rapids, MI: Zondervan Publishing House, 2002), 247.

Chapter 11—Giving Thanks Is Not Just for Thanksgiving

1. Sonja Lyubomirsky, *The How of Happiness* (New York: Penguin, 2007), 89.

2. Lyubomirsky, 93-95.

3. Joseph Linley, *Positive Psychology in Practice* (Hoboken, NJ: John Wiley & Sons, Inc., 2004), 474.

4. Michael J. Fox, *Always Looking Up: So Much to Be Grateful For* (excerpt in *Good Housekeeping* magazine, April 2009), 135.

5. Thomas Merton, *Thoughts in Solitude* (Boston: Shambhala Publications, 1986), 42.

6. Georgia Shaffer, *The Gift of Mourning Glories* (Grand Rapids, MI: Vine Books, 2000).

7. Lewis Smedes, as quoted by Don Postema, *Space for God* (Grand Rapids, MI: CRC Publications, 1997), 61.

8. For more teaching on cultivating humility, see my book *How to Find Selfless Joy in a Me-First World* (Colorado Springs, CO: WaterBrook Press, 2003).

9. Postema, 57.

10. Christopher Peterson, *A Primer in Positive Psychology* (Oxford, NY: Oxford University Press, 2006), 31.

11. Peterson, 33.

12. Peterson, 38.

13. Peterson, 38.

14. Henri J.M. Nouwen, *Henri Nouwen: Writings Selected with an Introduction by Robert A. Jonas* (Maryknoll, NY: Orbis Books, 1998), 69.

About the Author

Leslie Vernick is a licensed clinical social worker with a private counseling practice near Allentown, Pennsylvania. She is the author of *The Emotionally Destructive Relationship, Defeating Depression, How to Act Right When Your Spouse Acts Wrong,* and several other books. She has also contributed to the *Soul Care Bible, Competent Christian Counseling,* and numerous other books. She is an active member of the American Association of Christian Counselors and teaches in two of their video series: *Marriage Works* and *Extraordinary Women.*

Leslie and her husband, Howard, have been married for more than 30 years and are the proud parents of two grown children, Ryan and Amanda.

Leslie is a popular speaker at conferences, women's retreats, and couples' retreats. She loves to encourage and motivate people to deepen their relationship with God and others. For more information on Leslie's work and ministry, visit her Web site at www.leslievernick.com.

DEFEATING DEPRESSION
Real Hope for Life-Changing Wholeness

One woman in eight will experience clinical depression in her lifetime. The good—no, *great*—news is that there is hope. Real hope for permanent, life-changing wholeness.

Years of counseling experience, as well as her own battle with depression, allow Leslie Vernick to speak with extraordinary authority and compassion. She helps you...

- make sense of the symptoms of depression and what causes them
- hold on to God more firmly and trust that He won't abandon you
- listen to and grasp what your depression is revealing to you
- take specific steps to get better—and also grow stronger
- look forward to feeling normal again and enjoying the future

Don't give up on your life and dreams because of depression. Look to God, and with Him beside you and the love of your friends and family behind you, fight back and win!

To read an excerpt from *Defeating Depression,* see page 241 of this book.

The Emotionally Destructive Relationship
Seeing It, Stopping It, Surviving It

Stop. Dare to ask the question: *What's going wrong in this relationship?*

Maybe it doesn't seem to be "abuse." No bruises, no sexual violation. Even smiles on the surface. Nonetheless, before your eyes, a person is being destroyed emotionally. Perhaps that person is someone you want to help. Perhaps it's you.

Step by step, author and counselor Leslie Vernick guides you on how to...

- recognize behaviors that are meant to control, punish, and hurt
- confront and speak truth when the timing is right
- determine when to keep trying and when to shift your approach
- get safe and stay safe
- continue to be transformed by God

Do you want to change? Within the pages of this book, you will find biblically sound, straightforward help to take the first step now.

IF YOU HAVE ENJOYED *LORD, I JUST WANT TO BE HAPPY*,
YOU OR SOMEONE CLOSE TO YOU MAY ALSO FIND
ONE OF LESLIE VERNICK'S OTHER BOOKS HELPFUL.
FOLLOWING IS AN EXCERPT FROM *DEFEATING DEPRESSION*.

5

The Enemy Within

How precious are your thoughts about me, O God!
They are innumerable! I can't even count them;
They outnumber the grains of sand! And when I
wake up in the morning you are still with me!
PSALM 139:17-18 NLT

I, the LORD, speak the truth;
I declare what is right.
ISAIAH 45:19

For my fiftieth birthday, my friend Barb treated me to a private exercise session with her personal trainer. Prior to my individual time, the instructor invited us to participate in the class she was teaching. When I walked in, I immediately felt self-conscious. Mirrors circled an entire room filled with gorgeous young women who had toned bodies and wore the latest exercise fashions. I wore shorts and a T-shirt and felt old and frumpy. As we began to exercise, I focused on the teacher. I did not know this particular routine, and I needed to pay close attention. Whenever I glanced at the mirror and saw myself exercising, I was tempted to either laugh or cry. I looked so different than those lithe young bodies gracefully bending into the various poses. The more I kept my eyes glued on the teacher, the easier it became to focus on learning the technique. The longer I stared at myself with my imperfections, the more awful I felt.

Later on as I reflected on my morning, I realized that this was true of my inner life as well. The more I keep my eyes on Jesus, the more I will stay focused on what is true, good, and right. The more I gaze at myself in morbid introspection, the more self-conscious and depressed I will become.

Research on female mental health indicates that most women who experience depression also have poor self-esteem. Even women who don't feel particularly depressed say self-esteem and self-image problems are recurrent themes in their lives.

Why is this so? I believe one reason (of many) is that women tend to look at themselves through the mirror of their own eyes or the eyes of others, rather than through the eyes of God. When we regularly do that, we are always going to have a distorted picture of ourselves—one that will leave us feeling either vain and proud or discouraged and destroyed.

Women who are vain have inflated self-images and a great deal of self-esteem, often believing they are more important than others. On the other hand, women who see themselves negatively battle with anxiety, depressed moods, and feelings of worthlessness, inferiority, shame, and guilt. Those who think too much of themselves and those who think negatively of themselves have one thing in common: They are each centered on themselves rather than on Christ.

In order to understand how often we become our own worst enemy, let's first tackle what constitutes self-image and self-esteem, and then let's analyze what these things have to do with depression and good mental, spiritual, and relational health.

Understanding Self-Image and Self-Esteem

Our self-image is our mental picture of ourselves. Self-esteem is the way we feel about ourselves. When a woman says she has a poor self-image or low self-esteem, she usually means she doesn't like her-self and doesn't see herself as a lovable, competent, or worthwhile person. Subsequently, she doesn't feel good about herself. Each of us begins to form a picture of ourselves from birth as we get a sense of how we are received and valued by those around us.

Grinning from ear to ear, Joyce recently brought me some pho-tographs of her new granddaughter. "Isn't she beautiful?" she crooned. "Everyone is so taken with her." Baby Grace was the only girl born in several generations of children, so she became an instant celebrity.

Joyce provided the right opening to ask what her new little grand-child did to deserve such love and devotion. Puzzled, she answered, "Why would she have to do anything? She's my granddaughter. I love her just because."

Joyce gave a perfect answer to my question.

"And so," I continued, "if you, Joyce, being a mere human, can love baby Grace with such fervor, even though she cries and gets crabby and sometimes spits up all over you, why can't God love you just because?"

Joyce struggles with chronic depression and low self-esteem. Much of it has to do with the way she sees herself. Growing up, Joyce never felt loved or valued as a child. Her parents divorced when she was only five years old; her dad wasn't interested in her, and Joyce's mom was preoccupied with building a new life. Joyce's parents weren't abu-sive, just indifferent and busy. Joyce felt alone much of her childhood, and as a young girl she concluded she must not be worth anything and didn't deserve to be loved. She told herself that there must be something fundamentally undesirable about her that caused her par-ents to treat her with such neglect.

No one ever said such words directly to Joyce. Her conclusions about her value and worth came from her own perception of things as she saw herself through her parents' indifference. Joyce's picture of herself was understandable, but untrue. Her early neglect was real, but that didn't mean she was worthless or unlovable as a person, even if her parents didn't value her or love her the way she wanted them to, or even if they didn't love her at all. Rather, the situation said much more about the character of her parents and their own immaturity and sinful hearts. The consequences of her parents' sinful neglect, however, significantly impacted Joyce's life.

Looking at Joyce's early childhood, it isn't hard to see how those kinds of experiences would influence the way Joyce came to see herself (her self-image) as well as how she felt about herself (her self-esteem). Sadly, when we don't think we're worth anything to anyone and don't feel loved or important, we become a perfect candidate for depression as well as relationship problems.

Joyce's granddaughter, Grace, has the opportunity to get a different picture of herself from her first human relationships. Right from birth she is seeing herself as a much-loved and cherished child. She sees people smile at her and feels the love and warmth around her. When she cries, she is comforted and cared for. When she smiles, people who love her respond with jubilant glee. Her physical body is fed, diapered, hugged, and held. Before she can speak a word, she is forming a picture about herself that she is important and valuable to those around her and that she can trust them to care for her.

But no parents are perfect, and baby Grace is bound to experience some disappointments with the people in her world. Her parents won't always respond as quickly as she'd like when she cries. They will probably show some irritation or impatience in their voices or mannerisms when she acts crabby or whines. As Grace grows up and enters school, she won't always be treated fairly or favorably, nor will everyone always like her. What will Grace tell herself when someone doesn't think she's so cute or when she fails a test or is rejected or mocked by her friends?

Every child suffers the hard bumps that challenge a sense of worth, value, and competence. Rarely does anyone escape these years without a few deep wounds. How Grace sees herself in these experiences and then processes them in her heart will shape her mental and emotional picture of herself as well as her feelings about her abilities, value, and worth. God has charged parents with the responsibility to help their children work through these painful experiences using the wisdom he provides (see Deuteronomy 6 for an example). When that doesn't happen, or when a parent's own words or actions harm a child's spirit or body, a distorted self-image and poor self-esteem can be the result.

Consequences of a Distorted Self-Image and Poor Self-Esteem

Sometimes we mistakenly think that only those who think poorly of themselves have damaged self-images. On the contrary, many problems in life occur when we think too highly of ourselves and have an inflated self-esteem. Those who see themselves as more worthy, more special, and more deserving often treat others like second-class citizens and tend to have poor interpersonal relationships. These individuals believe that they are entitled to things that they are not entitled to and deserving of things they do not deserve. Our culture reinforces this kind of inflated thinking with the advertising slogans of "You deserve it" and "You're worth it."

When people around them don't treat them as they feel they deserve to be treated, they often become angry and depressed. A perfect example is the television reality program *American Idol*. Talented singers and people who want to be stars audition before three judges in hopes of becoming the next singing sensation. During the auditions, the judges shatter some of the contestants' dreams with the words, "You have the worst voice I have ever heard" or "That was terrible." Contestants who hold an inflated self-image express anger and disbelief, saying, "These judges don't know what they're talking about. Why don't they see my true worth and give me the chance that I deserve? I'm a great singer and could be the next American Idol." But everyone who heard the audition knows the real truth—although the judges could have been kinder with their words, their judgments were correct.

Sadly, people with an inflated view of themselves don't always allow the harsh corrections of reality to change their thinking in order for them to develop a more truthful view of themselves—a healthier self-image. As a result, they are often prone to feeling angry, disappointed with others, and sometimes depressed because everyone doesn't see them as wonderful or as desirable or as competent as they see themselves.

Whether we see ourselves too favorably or too negatively, having a distorted self-image is not only contrary to God's best for us, but also makes many women prone to depression. Let's look at some of the long-term consequences that occur when we fail to recognize and correct this problem.

Loss of One's True Self

A woman who views herself negatively tells herself that she doesn't matter or is not worthy of love. She often denies her true feelings, even to herself. One client, Sandy, kept telling me "It doesn't matter" when I asked her how she felt when her husband, a pastor, worked long, long hours in ministry. But I knew Sandy wasn't being honest, especially with herself. It's a short walk from "it doesn't matter" to "I don't matter," and that's what Sandy was really telling herself. Sandy feared admitting her true feelings. When she was finally able to express that she felt hurt, lonely, and angry, she quickly added, "But I feel guilty for feeling that way. I'm being selfish to want his time when there are so many people who need him more. He's doing God's work. Who am I to say he should work less hours just to spend time with me?"

Sandy distanced herself from her negative feelings because they were in opposition with another internal voice that told her she was selfish and wrong to feel them in the first place. Next, guilt and shame stepped in because now that she admitted having those feelings, she saw herself as a selfish and greedy person. With all this inner turmoil going on in Sandy's heart, over time she learned it was easier to squash her honest feelings and do what she thought was expected of her.

How we deal interpersonally with such dilemmas will be covered much more extensively in chapter 9. For now, understand that Sandy's way of seeing herself contributed to how she related to her husband, as well as to others in her life. Sandy will not be able to have a constructive discussion with her husband about what bothers her until she begins to give some credibility to her real feelings and learns to fight her harsh inner critic.

Like Sandy, many women lose who they are in the context of maintaining a relationship. Fear of rejection and fear of failure keep them from being honest with themselves and others. They worry that if they are honest, it will cost them the thing they value the most—their relationships. It's easier to go along—and go along—and go along—until they are so depressed they can't go along anymore.

Like Sandy, many women remind me of a chameleon. They always change colors to match their environment, adapting and becoming what they think others want them to be in order to gain someone's attention or secure their favor. They ask themselves, *Who should I be so I can be liked; or so that I will succeed; or so that I will be perceived as a worthy, lovable, and valuable person; or a person worth listening to and spending time with?*

When a woman doesn't see herself as worth anything, this strongly influences her style of relating. She no longer knows herself or expresses what she feels or wants. She is not growing to become what God wants her to become. Rather, she becomes an expert at knowing what other people want or expect and adapts herself to meet those expectations—losing her true self in the process.

> *I tried to be everything to everybody with no thought of myself at all. I had no "self," only the self others wanted me to be. This was played out in my need to please everyone, including people at work. I had no boundaries and allowed my company and church to pile more and more on me as a manager and as a worship leader until I broke down completely.* ~Laura

I am a perfectionist but never good enough. I am a people pleaser, but there's always someone who's unhappy with me. I don't know how to relate with others because I always want them to like me and don't care about what I want. In general, my depression exists because I have very low self-esteem and do things in my life that guarantee that self-esteem will stay low. I have not been able to unlearn that love is conditional and that "I am not worthy."
                                                          ~ Sarah

Negative Self-Evaluation

Another consequence of poor self-image and negative self-esteem is that we are constantly analyzing and scrutinizing ourselves, and we're never very positive with what we see. During my exercise class, when my eyes were on the mirror instead of my instructor, I found plenty to be unhappy about. My clothes were definitely out of style, my shape was rounder than I would have liked, I was one of the oldest women in the class, and my ability to perform the exercises was minimal. If I let all of those negative thoughts and feelings have free rein, I might have left the gym before I was finished, telling myself I was stupid to go or that I looked foolish. Thankfully, in that moment, I was able to laugh at myself, accepting myself as older and rounder than the other women in the class. I put my eyes right back on my instructor so I could learn the exercises and work toward getting in better shape.

Society exerts tremendous pressure on women to be thin as well as look beautiful and youthful. Billions of dollars are spent on cosmetic surgery to achieve the "ideal" face or body. Ordinary women will never measure up to these standards. Who can afford to? But if we always tell ourselves that we should be thinner or look younger or more beautiful, or when people in our lives reinforce these lies, then we will feel constantly disappointed and insecure with ourselves because we aren't or don't, and depression may be the result.

Christian culture has some unspoken expectations for women as well; for example, we should always be nice and never hurt anyone's feelings. We should always put other people's needs and wants ahead of our own, and we must never get loud or be pushy or bossy, even if we feel angry. We should keep a beautiful and orderly home, raise successful and godly children, achieve a meaningful career or ministry, have great girlfriends, *and* make our husband really happy. Whew! I'm worn out just writing it.

Poet May Sarton, who also battled depression, said,

> I think the secret of much of the unrest and dissatisfaction with one's self and longing for a more vivid, expressive existence is the thing planted deep in everyone— turning toward the sun, the love of a virtue and splendor that must be adored. One is always trying to tune one's self to an unheard perfection. Sadly, often the perfection we're trying to tune ourselves into is a false image of the perfect self instead of God.

When we measure our value and worth against our ability to maintain either our own or someone else's ideal standards, we will always fall short and suffer. No one ever stands next to "perfect" and feels good about being imperfect.

Every woman, even the one with a good self-image and positive self-esteem, battles her inner critic. Depressed women often lose this battle because the internal voice of depression is relentlessly cruel and colors her perspective on everything.

> *I make myself worse just by beating up on myself.*
> ~ Pamela

> *I was always telling myself all the wrong things in my life were my fault.* ~ Jean

> *I can't help but feel I am weak and can't cope on my own.*
> ~ Kim

I get negative toward myself. I let things linger and then explode. I get very low thinking of things from my past, what I could have done differently, or what more I could have done and can do. ~Rebekah

My depression made me feel worse. It made me feel I am a somewhat stupid person who has no place anywhere, not even at church or at work. It makes me feel like a worthless person. ~Shelly

My difficult marriage and children's problems contributed to me feeling overwhelmed, although the depression and feelings of worthlessness stem from me. I still tend to be a perfectionist and I am really hard on myself at times. I also believe things about myself that I shouldn't (I'm worthless, etc.) and lies from Satan, that I'm not really saved. ~Janet

The following statements are some typical things that I hear depressed women tell themselves:

- I'm a horrible mother/wife/sister/daughter/friend/Christian.
- I'm fat and ugly.
- I'm a loser.
- I'm not worth anything.
- I'm stupid.
- I can't do anything right.
- I'm a failure.
- I'm a fraud.
- I'm a disappointment to everyone.
- I'm a hypocrite.

- I'm no good.
- I never measure up.
- I'm helpless.
- I'm hopeless.

When a woman who already lives with a negative self-image and poor self-esteem gets depressed, these feelings intensify and can become unbearable. The most dangerous place a woman's cruel inner critic brings her to is to believe she is helpless to change anything and it's hopeless to try. Then suicide seems like a reasonable alternative to a lifetime of pain. If you recognize that you are at this place, please call someone to help you. These feelings are too powerful for you to battle alone, and the consequences too grave if you fail. Tell your husband, pastor, best friend, a counselor, or your medical doctor, or call your local crisis hotline.

The remedy for the person with a negative self-image, as well as the person with an inflated self-image, is truth. God's Word tells us not to misjudge our value and worth, but to see ourselves truthfully—as God sees us (see Romans 12:3).

The most important question we must ask ourselves is not how I got this way, but how can I change so that I will see myself and my situations from God's perspective?

Seeing Ourselves Truthfully

We have heard this word "truth" many times thus far. That's because it is the only medicine that will heal our wounded, depressed, and sin-sick heart. Medicine is only able to do its work if we take it, and even then it usually doesn't heal us instantly. Absorbing the medicine of truth takes time. Please be patient with yourself. God knows that pure truth is often too potent to be administered alone. Truth must always be mixed with grace and love, and the Lord usually gives us small amounts of truthful medicine to start. Just as we need to take certain medicines for the rest of our lives, the healing elixir of truth isn't only taken when we're sick. We need daily doses of it to help us stay healthy and grow.

The Bible says that our heart automatically leans toward believing lies over truth (Jeremiah 8:5; 17:9; Romans 1:25). We don't intentionally plant lies in our heart, but like weeds in our flower garden, they are there. And just as weeds mar the beauty of a garden, lies and deception (whether it be self-deception or lies told to us) ruin a soul. In his bestselling book *The Road Less Traveled,* psychiatrist Scott Peck said, "One of the roots of mental illness is invariably an interlocking system of lies that we have been told and lies we tell ourselves."

When we believe lies about ourselves, lies about God, lies about life, lies about how to handle problems, and lies about others, we become mentally, emotionally, and spiritually ill. To become healthy, we must first identify these lies and then renounce them for what they are. This process needs to be done regularly because, like weeds, many lies we have believed have deep roots that are not easily killed.

As we grow to see things more truthfully about ourselves, God, others, and life, the next step is figuring out how to live in that different reality. For example, how do I live as a woman of dignity and value? How should I handle myself when I fail or disappoint myself? How do I speak the truth in love to others when they hurt me? How do I draw close to God when I no longer see him as a harsh judge or as a disinterested Deity, but rather as a loving Father who enjoys me? Learning to believe these truths is the first step; living from them takes time and practice. As in most other things, the more consistently we apply what we are learning to real-life situations, the more we will gain confidence and become better with those situations.

God's Word is the only true mirror that accurately reflects who we are and how we are to see ourselves. Just as I needed to stop staring at myself in the mirror and keep my eyes on my exercise instructor in order to stay focused and make progress, we need to keep our eyes on God and his Word as our means of seeing ourselves and our situation truthfully. The battle you face right now is which voice you will listen to and trust to be your truest truth. Will it be God's Word or the negative voices in your own head and heart? The following truth is foundational in starting to correct your self-image:

> **God loves you because he chooses to,**
> **not because you are worthy of his love or deserve it.**

At first glance, this may sound shocking to those of us who have been fed a steady diet of psychobabble, but in reality, once you grasp this truth, it is quite freeing. Authentic love is always a gift, not a reward for good behavior or something we can earn.

Many depressed women say, "I wish I could believe God loves me, but I can't because I don't feel worthy. Help me feel worthy." The internal lie is *I must be or feel worthy in order to receive love.* This is a common deception in depression as well as in women with low self-esteem. We all want to feel worthy and deserving. That would make us feel good about ourselves and boost our sagging self-images. Here's one woman's struggle to get free from this lie:

> *I believe that God is loving and forgiving and that*
> *nothing I have done or will do can change that. I believe*
> *that my name is in the "Book of Life," but I'd rather keep*
> *proving that I am worthy enough to be there for some*
> *reason. Old habits!* ~ Sarah

Let's first take a look at this lie on the human level. Do we love our children because they deserve to be loved or are worthy of it? If the answer is yes, we love them *because* they are worthy and deserving, then what about those children who aren't loved? The day after Joyce shared with me the good news about her granddaughter, another baby girl washed up dead on the New Jersey shore. Was Grace *more* worthy to be loved than that abandoned infant? Absolutely not! Every child is a gift from God and should be received and valued as such. If someone gives me a diamond bracelet and I throw it in the trash, does that act make the bracelet less valuable? No, it makes me a fool.

Along the same line, my husband, Howard, does not love me because I deserve it. In fact, many times I don't deserve his love. He loves me because he wants to, not because I'm worthy. And if he didn't want to love me someday, it would not be because I was no longer worthy. My worth has nothing to do with it. Love is a choice. It cannot be coerced or forced, bought or earned. It is a gift from the one who loves to the beloved. In the Bible the stories of Hosea and Gomer (see the Old Testament book of Hosea) and the prodigal son (Luke 15:11-32) richly demonstrate how *undeserving* the one who is loved can be. Love cannot be something that is deserved, otherwise it isn't genuine love.

It's true that people don't always love us the way we'd like them to or as much as we want them to. Rejection hurts, but rejection is not a statement about our true worth or value. Let's look at this from a slightly different angle. Suppose I went around telling everyone who didn't love me the way I'd like them to that I deserved to be loved and valued by them because I was worthy and deserving of it. Love never works that way. I think if I acted like that, everyone would rightly think I was quite full of myself and be turned off.

Perhaps someone you loved told you that you were a burden or a mistake. Careless words wound a person's spirit and can be extremely painful. But please hear me. *Even if your parents or your husband or everyone you know treated you horribly, you are still a person of value. You have eternal significance.* How do I know this? Because your heavenly Father, your Creator, God Almighty, declares this to be so (Matthew 10:31; 12:12; Ephesians 2:10). He loves you fully and completely—not because you are cute or talented or perfect or worthy. He loves you because he chooses to love you.

⌒